The One-Hour Orgasm™

Also by Bob Schwartz, Ph.D.

Diets Don't Work™

Diets Still Don't Work™

Self-Talk for Weight Loss (coauthor)

Also by Leah Schwartz, Ph.D.

Who Taught You That?: Answers to 101 Important Questions About Sex

FunGasms!™*: The Ultimate Guide to Having Fun Every Day!* (coauthor)

The One-Hour Orgasm™

How to Learn the Amazing "Venus Butterfly"™ Technique

LEAH SCHWARTZ, PH.D., AND

BOB SCHWARTZ, PH.D.

St. Martin's Griffin

NEW YORK

www.stmartins.com

Library of Congress Cataloging-in-Publication Data

Schwartz, Bob.
The one-hour orgasm : how to learn the amazing "Venus Butterfly" technique / by Robert M. Schwartz and Leah M. Schwartz.
p. cm.
ISBN-13: 978-0-312-35919-5
ISBN-10: 0-312-35919-5
1. Sex instruction. 2. Orgasm. I. Title.

HQ31 .S414 1999
613.9'6—dc21

99091165

First published in the United States by Breakthru Publishing

10 9 8 7 6 5 4

Acknowledgments

First and foremost, profound thanks to:

Dr. W. Victor Baranco (1934–2002), educator and founder of the More Philosophy, to whose memory this book is dedicated. Without his phenomenal wisdom and insight into human sexuality, this book would not have been possible. Though Dr. Baranco is no longer with us, his words continue to provide inspiration and guidance. Equally, for their generosity and graciousness, thanks to Drs. Cynthia Baranco and Suzanne Baranco, who were active partners in his lifelong research.

Walter Maksym and Satoko Kitamura for your insightful contributions to the writing and updating of this edition, your dear friendship, love, endless support, courage, and passion to keep the vision alive and available to the world.

Special thanks to:

Janet O'Neal for your unconditional love, support, and wisdom that helped make this book the best it could be. Jack Mayer for your total commitment to excellence in designing the original covers, layout, type, and final editing of the original editions. Frank Reuter, Ph.D. for your honesty and efforts in editing the original editions. Jennifer Weis and Stefanie Lindskog, the St. Martin's Press editors, for contributing their insightfulness and expertise in making this edition possible.

All of the DJ and radio/TV talk show hosts, *and their open-minded producers,* who were so very brave to share the valuable information contained in this book with their audiences. Universal Pictures for featuring *The One Hour Orgasm*™ in their blockbuster movie, *Meet the Fockers. Mad Magazine* for their parody of *Meet the Fockers* and *The One Hour Orgasm*™.

Peter Miller, the "Literary Lion," for all your magnificent "roars" in producing the "orgasmic deal" that made the republication of this book by St. Martin's Press a reality!

Important Note to Readers

This book is a starting point only . . . but it has been the authors' fondest hope that it will be the beginning of an exciting, fulfilling, and pleasurable journey. To best ensure that you use this information as intended by the authors and the publisher, please read this note carefully.

First, this material is intended for a mature audience. Before reading on, please be advised that this book includes graphic photographs and diagrams, including nudity, used to illustrate the information provided in the text. If for any reason this sort of material isn't appropriate for you, please do not read on.

Also, the material in this book is based upon years of formal and informal study and observation by the authors, including decades of work with couples and individuals, and reflects their strongly held viewpoints and opinions based on this study and observation. This material is intended as coaching on the topic of pleasure and is offered for informational and educational purposes only. It is not intended as medical or psychotherapeutic advice or in any manner intended to diagnose, treat or serve as a prescription for any medical condition, illness, or disease, nor is it intended in any way to replace the advice of your medical doctor, therapist, or other health care professional. And the authors are not, nor do they claim to be, licensed medical doctors, psychiatrists or health professionals of any kind. Rather, they have Ph.D.s in lifestyles and sensuality, respectively. And, while this book is designed to offer accurate current information, research and knowledge about health issues is constantly evolving. **If you or your partner have a physical, mental, or emotional condition that might be affected by sexual or other physical activity, or which might interfere with your abilities to relate in any way, or if you have any questions or concerns about your physical, emotional, or mental health, you should consult a physician or**

other appropriate health care professional before following any of the suggestions in this book. This includes seeking appropriate professional advice regarding any concerns about practicing safer sex. Practicing safer sex and reducing the risks of sexually transmitted diseases are important practices for anyone who is sexually active. Readers are urged to use common sense and keep in mind that all intimate and sexual contact involves inherent risks, including health and disease risks and the risk of pregnancy. **The safer sex practices discussed in this book are intended to encourage safer sex, but are not, and should not be considered, a substitute for medical advice.** The only way to ensure absolute safety in the context of sexual relations is abstinence; no assurances or guarantees of any kind are given to the reader that the safer sex practices suggested in this book will prevent STD or HIV transmission.

Finally, references in this book to products and potential sources of additional information does not mean that the authors, the publisher, or anyone else associated with the publishing of this book, respectively, endorses, or is responsible for, such products or the information or recommendations in such sources. (For example, the fact that the authors' Web site is listed does not mean that the publisher endorses any of the information provided there, nor does the fact that a product is mentioned in this book or on the authors' Web site mean that the publisher endorses that product.)

Foreword

My encounters with Dr. Bob Schwartz and Dr. Victor Baranco and their lives' work profoundly transformed the quality of my life.

Before meeting Bob and Vic I was well educated and successful, but the acquired skills that had served me so well in the world utterly failed me in my intimate life. I could have never grasped, in the absence of those encounters, the possibility of having a phenomenally great sensual life, let alone "winning" with women. What was worse, I didn't know that such a possibility existed. Indeed, from my experiences, education, and enculturation such a prospect seemed quite impossible, or at the least, given my Chicago-Midwest upbringing, California "woo-woo."

Then, I had the unexpected good fortune of meeting Bob, who, in turn, introduced me to Vic. Thereafter, I had the pleasure and privilege to come to know Bob, Vic, and their visions while representing them and California's More University and Institute for Human Abilities, founded by Vic, as clients. Dear friendships developed. They were gentle but enormously powerful men possessed of genuine horse sense, humor, and insightful brilliance who shared themselves lovingly, enthusiastically, and "selfishly for their own pleasure," making sure to never lose sight of the goal—fun! Their unique way of being moved, touched and inspired me by interacting with me in such a way that I could provide for myself the opportunity to create, for the first time, an entirely new way of seeing and a structure for interpreting my universe and everything in it, including myself, in a way that was gratifying at all levels of my existence. It was my privilege and pleasure to know them.

As coauthors, but most importantly, as soul mates, Bob and Leah wrote this book as a loving collaboration when he responded to her "call" to join her in sharing this valuable information with the world. Dr. Leah, the love of Bob's life, and he hers, inspired him to produce this book for her pleasure! You are about to become the beneficiary of that "call" and Bob's enthusiastic response to it. They had, as did Vic and his wife, Dr. Cynthia Baranco, the most amazing, fun, man-woman relationships I had ever encountered. That same possibility can be seized by you, here and now, though their words.

When Bob departed this life in 2001 and Vic in 2002, I lost two of my dearest friends, men who had become my gurus, heros, partners, and brothers. Yet, I rejoice for them because, unlike so many, they had no regrets when they were done. They thoroughly enjoyed experiencing every moment of their lives right down to the last as right and were 100 percent complete when it was their time to go. Inspired by their enthusiasm, courage, and example to find themselves, others, life,—indeed, everything right and perfect, doubt their doubts, and put good in the world, it is now my privilege to stand on their shoulders and share their work with the world through this fourth revised edition. We've updated Bob and Leah's first person rendition only to the degree necessary to assure it lives on in a way that continues to capture and deliver their loving collaboration, as it did when it first rolled off the press.

My appreciation to Dr. Leah, who, in her ongoing commitment to continue to share her and her late husband's and Vic and Cindy's vision, has granted me the rare opportunity to contribute to the writing of this edition and to make this book even more widely available. Hopefully, your encounter with their "More Philosophy" and associated sensual methodology will make a difference for you, too, by expanding your sexual potential and capacity to have more fun experiencing, producing, and creating a more satisfying, pleasurable life for yourself and others.

What you will learn by undertaking the adventure of reading this book you will not likely find anywhere else. Just start by finding what you have now right, good, and perfect, doubt the doubt, don't forget to do your "homework," and experience what occurs. As you will see, this book does not merely reveal techniques.

Rather, it reveals a powerful way of relating to yourself and others that may lead you to discover that "One Hour" is only the beginning and that much, much "more" lies beyond. I therefore invite you to begin your journey of possibility and pleasure by turning the page. I trust you will have fun reading this enlightening gem of a book!

—Walter Maksym
Chicago, Illinois
March 2006

Introduction

Most people, no matter what their sexual experience, don't believe that orgasms that can last for up to an hour are possible for a normal man or woman. Neither did we. Even if you *could* learn how to give longer and more intense orgasms, why would anyone be interested? You won't ask that question after you and your partner master the "Venus Butterfly" technique.

The good news is that you are about to discover that the value of this book goes far beyond the promise of the title. ***The One Hour Orgasm*** is based on over 30 years of research and courses taught at More University and The Institute of Human Abilities in northern California.

Following are some of the benefits you can expect from reading this book.

If you are a woman:

- Learn how to initiate sex and turn him on without any effort on his part.
- Increase the strength and duration of his erections.
- Train his sexual nervous system to last longer.
- Increase the intensity and length of his orgasms.
- Increase the amount of fun you both have in the bedroom.
- Learn how to add 1 to 3 inches to his normal size.
- Improve your self-confidence as a lover.

If you are a man:

- Understand how to thoroughly satisfy your partner every time.
- Increase the frequency of love-making by making sex better for her.

- Make every love-making session a pleasurable learning experience.
- Solve the common problem of not being in the mood at the same time.
- Increase the intensity and duration of her orgasms.
- Eliminate boredom and increase the fun you both have in the bedroom.
- Learn how to get her in the mood without any effort on her part.
- Make as little as one inch feel like twelve inches to her.
- Bring back her sex drive or prevent it from ever going away.
- Improve your self-confidence as a lover.

Tens of thousands of people have benefited from the sexual and relationship skills that are taught in the courses at More University and The Institute of Human Abilities and, now, so can you.

Our Story

Our own excitement about the importance of the information in this book has come a long way from how it started out.

In 1986, when we first learned of the sexual techniques being taught in the courses at More University and The Institute of Human Abilities in California, we were not interested. We had been together for nine years and felt that our sex life was better than good. Even though the frequency of our love making had gone down slightly over those years, we were convinced that it was still one of the best parts of our relationship.

However, many of our friends began to "modestly" brag about the results—both inside and outside of the bedroom—they had achieved from taking a few of the courses. Not only did they claim that sex for them had improved immensely, but because of their improved relationship with each other, they were also rapidly reaching many of their personal and professional goals. Some of the women had even lost noticeable weight without dieting.

This last curious side benefit is what got our attention. It had taken us over twenty years of study and research to write and publish our *New York Times* Best-Selling book, *Diets Don't Work* (www.dietsdontwork.net), which helps people with weight problems or eating disorders lose weight by teaching them the secrets we learned from studying "naturally thin" people. Yet here was some university teaching people how to have better sex, and some of them were losing weight without even reading our book.

Neither of us liked the idea of going to a "sex" course. On the other hand, a lot of people we respected, plus thousands of others, were raving about the results they had achieved from the courses.

A "Basic Sensuality 101" course was being held on the weekend after Thanksgiving Day. We called and luckily got in at the last minute. Our lives have never been the same.

The information we learned has strengthened the very roots of our lives and our already successful relationship as we feel it will yours. It made such a positive difference in our relationship and sex life, we had to tell others about it.

Dr. Bob Schwartz
Dr. Leah Schwartz

Table of Contents

The One Hour Orgasm™

How to Learn the Amazing "Venus Butterfly"™ Technique

Chapter One

A What?

"A ***one hour*** orgasm! Is this a joke?," asked a friend when we told him what we were working on.

No.

A "one hour orgasm" is an orgasm with hundreds, even thousands, of orgasmic contractions one after the other after the other.

You don't believe this is possible? Join the club. Neither did we. No one we had ever met, including Dr. Ruth, had any idea of what we were talking about. The only way you will become a believer is the way we did. After your first one.

Do You Really Know What an Orgasm Is?

Most men and women, including many sex and relationship experts, seem to be very confused about what an orgasm actually is.

Most of them talk and act as if the ejaculation phase is the orgasm. This is not accurate, even for men. Of course, if that were true, women would never have them.

The most obvious signs of orgasm for both men and women are the orgasmic contractions which produce the intense pleasurable feelings which shoot those "wonderful-out-of-control" feelings throughout your whole mind and body.

The beginning phase of an orgasm starts when your genital area is feeling better than any other part of your body! If the pleasure you are experiencing continues and builds up, the sensations becomes stronger. These wonderful feelings usually begin to create mild orgasmic contractions. The orgasmic contractions can continue to build in intensity. They soon seem to take over your whole body and finally you feel as if you have come into contact with a cosmic light socket.

Have You Ever Counted Them?

During what most people consider a normal orgasm, men generally have 6 to 9 orgasmic contractions, each contraction lasting for approximately 8/10ths of a second. These contractions in a man are followed by the ejaculation of semen.

According to our research, only one out of three women had often, if ever, experienced orgasm through intercourse, but when they do, they have, on the average, 9 to 12 orgasmic contractions. Each contraction lasts for the same 8/10ths of a second that the man experiences.

One woman in a study we read had 33 orgasmic contractions, but they wrote her off because they thought her sexual nervous system had malfunctioned.

Bliss Is Closer Than You Think

As did thousands of other students, we learned the "Venus Butterfly" technique at More University and The Institute For

Human Abilities in California, where "Basic Sensuality 101" has been taught for over 30 years.

At the Institute, they call the 6 to 12 orgasmic contractions of a typical orgasm a "genital sneeze." It is not that sneezes are bad, it is just that they have discovered that a whole lot more is available with some education and a little homework.

Being able to produce a *one hour orgasm* means that you have mastered the "Venus Butterfly" technique in this book. Once you have practiced enough, you will be able to produce hundreds and hundreds of orgasmic contractions in your partner, man or woman.

Sound impossible? You won't see this in the *Guiness Book of World Records*, but the longest a woman's orgasm was kept going at More University was 11 hours! (Please don't try this at home. These were trained professionals and it was done only as a scientific experiment...not for fun.)

The good news is that after over 30 years of research, the researchers at More University and The Institute of Human Abilities still can't say what the upper limits of pleasure are that you can give your partner or that you can experience. With this new information you will:

- Have more confidence in bed
- Be able to increase the intensity and duration of your partner's orgasm
- Have more fun together as a couple
- Put the spark back into your relationship or keep it from going away
- Eliminate boredom and increase the fun you both have in the bedroom
- Learn something new that makes a big difference in your sex life and relationship
- Solve the common problem of not being in the mood at the same time
- Learn how to talk to each other about one of the most emotionally charged subjects in the world... sex!
- Bring back his (or her) sex drive

- Learn how to solve the two biggest problems men face today without drugs—his occasional or often inability to have or maintain an erection and pre-mature ejaculation
- Make every love-making session a pleasurable learning experience
- ***Even lose weight!***

Ask yourself this question: When was the last time you or your partner learned something new that improved your sex life and was so incredible that you continued to use it?

That time has come!

Chapter Two

What Is The "Venus Butterfly"?

The "Venus Butterfly" is not a sex toy or mechanical device. The "Venus Butterfly" is a sexual technique and philosophy for pleasure beyond your wildest dreams. It teaches you exactly when, where, and how to give your partner the most pleasure possible for the longest period of time.

As we will soon prove to you, the "Venus Butterfly" technique can be learned with a little instruction and practice by any man or woman. It is the key to having orgasmic contractions that last for up to an hour.

The most important benefit of the "Venus Butterfly" technique is that, unlike any other sexual technique, if done properly, it will totally gratify any man or woman every time.

This is what makes it the most effective and wonderful sexual technique ever taught.

The "Venus Butterfly" has all the advantages of every other sexual technique with few of the disadvantages. The importance of these advantages and disadvantages will become clear by the time you finish the book.

If you follow the simple, step-by-step, instructions we give you, without stopping too long between steps, you will see for yourself that the promises of the book are true.

Of course, if you want, you can skip around, ignore the instructions, or leave out parts. The problem is that if you do not follow the recipe exactly, you will most likely not wind up with the results we have promised.

Our goal is for you to have as much fun as possible as you try out the "Venus Butterfly" technique for yourself. Remember, nothing in this book is intended to do anything other than make your sex life and your relationship better than it is now.

A Man's Biggest Challenge

During our years of study, research, and teaching, we have discovered that some people have deep seated resistance when it comes to following instructions. For instance, it is hard for many men to admit that there is anything that they could learn that would increase their ability to sexually gratify a woman. On the other hand, one of a man's constant challenges is to be able to satisfy and please the woman he loves every time.

What makes the man's situation worse is that when women hear about *The One Hour Orgasm* and the "Venus Butterfly" technique, most are usually elated. She likes the idea that she also will be gratified each time they make love and that longer, more intense, and consistent orgasms are possible for her if he follows our instructions.

On the other hand a man's anxiety level sometimes goes up. It has been hard enough to get her to have a normal orgasm. Now he fears that she is going to expect to be gratified for an hour every time!

Relax. Just follow the instructions and you will be able to perform better and produce amazing results.

Notes

Chapter Three

What You Didn't Know That You Didn't Know

The first step in learning to master the "Venus Butterfly" technique is to introduce you to some information which is neither understood or known by very many people. It will answer a lot of questions that have puzzled the human race for thousands of years.

For instance, if you are a man, have you ever performed in a certain way in bed with your partner so that she was totally gratified? Then, maybe just a week later, you performed exactly the same way and the love making session was a dud for her.

What happened? You are pretty sure you did the same things, but you wound up with an entirely different result. The following information will clear up this and many other mysteries for you.

The Secret Word For Giving a Woman the Most Pleasure Possible: "Tumescence"

The first new thing I learned at More University and The Institute of Human Abilities is that only women have what can be accurately described as heat cycles. "So what?," I thought to myself, not realizing at that time that female sexual cycles are a source of enormous power. It is a power that needs to be understood and mastered in order to have relationships and sexual experiences beyond your present reality.

O.K., O.K.. My wife and all other women have monthly cycles (I knew that!) and even yearly cycles (I *didn't* know that).

One of the main reasons I married my wife, Leah, was that she was so nice. Leah was the first person who read the initial manuscript for my first book which we would eventually title, *Diets Don't Work.* By applying the principles in the book and learning to eat like a "naturally thin person" again, her weight declined and she got to her ideal weight...without dieting or depriving herself of anything that she wanted to eat.

This was when I fell in love with her. Anyone who listens to you, approves of everything you do, and is so very nice, is not a person you want to let get away. So, I asked her to marry me.

After that, especially around the time of her periods, I began to notice that Leah got slightly meaner and meaner as each month passed. The longer we were married, the meaner she seemed to get.

No matter what I came up with to soothe her, I always felt something was missing. I tried to reason with her. Sometimes I would hide from her. Other times I would try to do something to make her laugh or I would buy her presents. I tried to find a medicine that would "cure" her. When all else failed, we had big fights. Nothing seemed to work.

I began to keep track of when the "Alien" would arrive each month. This technique seemed to help a little, but not quite enough. Everything negative was exaggerated during this time and if I was ready for the attack…if I could convince her that it was her hormones this time and not me...,if...,if only she were more like a man.

Now I am glad that I did not get my stupid wish. What I was viewing as negative energy was actually the power source that keeps the human race on the planet. I did not know it at the time, but it was also the chief energy source of our exceptional love life.

At More University and The Institute for Human Behavior, this type of energy is called "Tumescence" (Tu-mess-ence). One of the definitions in the dictionary explains tumescence as "being swollen (as with sexual energy). (Sexual) Tension that is not being released or used."

For our purpose, this definition has been expanded to create some new distinctions that will help you to produce more pleasure and intensity in your love life. We will use this new word to describe a condition and a certain behavior that mammals, including humans, especially females, occasionally exhibit.

Our expanded definition of tumescence includes, among other things, the experience of being sexually aroused, or turned on. This can mean either an agitated state of mind or a very pleasant feeling of being sexually aroused. Tumesced* (pronounced tu-messed) can also mean a particular type of tension, similar to a rubber band that is being twisted tighter and tighter.

*From this point on, we will use this spelling and pronunciation for ease of reference. A more accurate spelling might be "tumefied" or "tumid," but those spellings sound too much like something you would do to an Egyptian mummy and have proven awkward when we have tried to use them.

The Signs of Tumescence

Tumescent energy can feel like a warm glow, one time and a raging fire the next.

The exciting news is that when tumescent energy is under control and channeled pleasurably, it can produce wonderful feelings and inspire everyone, especially men, to high levels of fun and even production.

Bitchiness

Tumescence has many forms. Tumescent (tu-mess-ent) energy is most commonly identified in the form of bitchiness or tension, as if the person were agitated by something or someone and all negative feelings are being magnified.

At other times, however, when the tumescent energy is at a lower level and under control, the person feels pleasantly aroused and positive feelings are intensified.

When To Look Out For Tumescence

First, it is important to understand that women have heat cycles twice a month and also seasonal heat cycles that show up twice a year.

The monthly cycles come around the time of ovulation and menstruation, and the seasonal heat cycles come in the spring and the fall.

Somewhere around three days before a woman's ovulation time, her tumescent energy or heat level starts to build up. After ovulation the level goes back down. Then about five days before her period, this tumescent energy or heat level begins its highest climb. Usually she grows more and more tumescent as she gets closer to the time of her period.

During her period, the tumescence begins to subside until around the time of her next ovulation cycle when it starts to increase again. Another tidal wave of energy begins to again build up power.

Historically, women have been misunderstood and mistreated when it comes to their tumescence or heat cycles. There are times they probably would like to deny they even have them.

Nearly all of us know that women are usually the most tumesced close to the time of their periods. Less than tasteful stories have been made up about this time, such as the one which says that if the shadow of a woman on her period falls on a snake, the snake will die.

No wonder women feel discriminated against and don't want to acknowledge their tumescent cycles. For years some medical doctors refused to believe that there was any such thing as PMS. Other physicians called it an illness, gave drugs to try to "cure" it, and even operated to get rid of the symptoms. Most of the treatments were designed to try to flatten the woman's highs and lows, to make her more "stable." In other words, to try to make her more like a man.

It is lucky that these physicians failed in their attempts because to try to make women more like men would be a great waste of potential fun and sexual energy. Instead of trying to eliminate the dynamic energy that women have, wouldn't it be a good idea to learn how to use it to increase the pleasure, productivity, and joy in our lives and relationships? That is one of the purposes of this book.

How Do You Spot Tumescence?

What are the signs of tumescence? Of course, crankiness or meanness are the major signs, but there are many other signals that are useful if you become familiar with them.

Tumescence is easiest to recognize in the form of anger, agitation, irritability, or being lustful, passionate, or highly sensitive. A tumesced person can also exhibit signs of clumsiness, lack of concentration, and disorientation.

The higher the level of tumescence and the longer it is sustained, the more radical the behavior usually becomes.

The Five Levels Of Tumescence

Tumescence can exhibit a multitude of different characteristics and intensify either positive or negative feelings depending upon the circumstances and the amount of tumescent energy that is present.

With ***The One Hour Orgasm***, we have created a scale from "1" to "5" to relate to tumescence. You can use these new distinctions to begin to recognize and deal with tumescent energy.

Level "1" is "flat." There is no sexual interest. All tumescent energy has been discharged. She feels mellow and totally relaxed.

Level "2" is when she is "a little turned on"...things are starting to get interesting. She is looking forward with slight anticipation.

Level "3" is when tumescent energy feels under control or if there are good and immediate prospects for releasing it. She is feeling a glow, turned-on, pleasantly excited. Tumescence at this level can feel extremely enjoyable. She feels pleasantly vulnerable, and, maybe even, emotionally mushy.

Level "4" is when she could start to get anxious, highly emotional, hot and bothered, on edge, irritable, or cranky. At this level tumescent energy begins to magnify feelings, no matter if they are positive or negative. For example, the hottest sex is available at this level and, on the other hand, a couple may have their biggest fights at level four or above.

Level "5" is when tumescence has built up too high. She feels out of control, desperate, frantic, hostile, hypercritical, or bad tempered. She may scream or snarl a lot at this level. She does not look or feel attractive, and will predictably behave somewhat irrationally and aggressively. High levels of tumescence, with no hope of relief in sight, can make a woman feel very uncomfortable with feelings of overwhelming pressure and even painful cramps.

The person feeling high tumescence can many times seem to be illogical, righteous, and unreasonable. She might thrash around feeling very uncomfortable and try desperately not to feel the feelings she is having.

She will usually try to figure out what is causing these unpleasant feelings. If her man is anywhere in the vicinity, he often seems like the cause of her suffering.

Most men have no idea how to even bring up the subject of tumescence, much less know how to handle it. Not knowing what to do when tumescent energy showed up was only one of the ways I came to find that, like other men, I was dumb when it came to women.

If your partner is at a level "1" and is feeling no sexual desire at all, it might be a good idea for you to start by learning how to raise her level of tumescence.

If your partner is at a level "5" and very agitated, it would serve you both well if you learned how to effectively bring her tumescence down as much as possible so that she will feel less pressure, stress, and tension.

People Who Live And Play Together, Tumesce Together

Women who work or live together for a while usually begin to have their cycles at the same time. If this tumescent energy builds up too high and is not acknowledged and discharged in a pleasurable or consciously directed way, it begins to cause problems for the person who is feeling it and almost everyone else around her.

Can Men Become Tumesced?

Yes, of course. Tumescence has the amazing characteristic of being the kind of energy which you can pick up from someone else.

Can a woman intentionally or unintentionally tumesce a man? Of course.

Have you ever noticed that men can become awkward or clumsy around a woman, especially if they find her attractive? And, if a man is around a highly agitated woman, does he become agitated? Yes. Yes. Yes.

Men Feel Bad Sometimes, Too!

Though men get tumesced, they don't appear to be affected by tumescence to the degree that a woman does.

If you are a man, just imagine being extremely agitated. What if you had been that way for three days, non-stop, with no relief, and none in sight? What might your outlook on life be, and is it possible that you might be caught looking around for someone to blame or take it out on?

What we have just described is a condition many women report experiencing frequently. What if a man felt restless, edgy, ugly, bloated, unloved, misunderstood, ignored, and agitated a couple of times a month? Is it possible he might become a little unreasonable sometimes? Would he possibly allow himself to feel better by being pampered a little? Do you think it might be illogical if he went shopping and even bought something because it made him feel better?

We know this concept of tumescence is strange at first, but we want you to go along with the notion for a few days and begin to look at your life using this idea.

Unless you first learn to recognize and deal with this particular type of energy, consistent, maximum, sexual pleasure and one hour orgasms are not easily attained. The good news is that, if you know how, you can increase or decrease this tumescent energy in yourself or others at will.

See if you can begin to notice how tumescence affects you and those around you.

Can you think of just one very recent incident in your life that may have been influenced by tumescence? It may have been a big or little fight. It could also have been a very pleasurable encounter. Use the space below to write down any specific details that you recall. Start with who you assume was generating the tumescent energy and then write out what happened.

____

____

____

____

The Source Of The Popular Male Impotency "Myth"

If you have ever been around an older male dog, you will see an example of a male mammal picking up tumescent signals from a female. The dog lays around, sleeps a lot, and looks very bored. A female dog in heat comes into the picture and suddenly you have an alert, excited, turned on, and happy puppy on your hands.

Men, and all male mammals, respond to being around and paying attention to a female who is turned on.

Whether they realize it or not, men are able to pick up and respond to a woman's heat cycle signals.

If a man is even thinking about sex, it is usually because he has received a transmitted feeling, intentional or not, that started in a woman.

It doesn't make any difference whether the woman is young or old, whether she has had a hysterectomy or not, nor does it make any difference if she is fat or thin.

She may not even be interested in doing anything with his turned on state of mind and body. She may enjoy testing out her ability to attract a man every once in a while just to make sure that her "equipment" is still working.

The Perfect Male?

A story about another mammal, the male Panda bear, demonstrates one more example of the reach, power, and existence of tumescent energy. The male Panda spends much of his time up in some bamboo tree, calmly munching on bamboo leaves.

Once every one to seven years or even longer, the female Panda gets turned on and is interested in sex. According to the story, she can be as far as twenty miles away, and yet the male Panda somehow senses her change of condition and runs through the forest until he finds her. They mate and then the male Panda returns to his bamboo tree to once again munch leaves and wait.

Male Impotency

Of course, men are not bears or dogs, but, we are mammals. If you begin to pay attention to the evidence of female tumescence around you, it will become clearer that women are the source of male sexual excitement and turn on.

This idea of who turns on who is contrary to what most of us have been brought up to believe. It goes against the popular assumption that men cause their own erections and are the sexual aggressors and women put up with men's sexual appetites.

The notion that men cause their own erections is one of the major reasons thirty million American men suffer from the fear of the occasional or frequent inability to have or maintain an erection.

The bottom line is this. A man generally cannot become aroused unless he has been around a woman who was aroused first. Of course, he can try to pretend or fantasize that some woman is turned on that he is thinking about and that she wants him to have sex with her. Another way he may be able to artificially manufacture an erection is to be touched or by touching himself in a pleasurable way.

This Is Just A Test

Try this fifteen second experiment with yourself (if you are a guy) or ask your man to try this (if you are a woman.)

Without using fantasy, have him snap his fingers and have an erection appear by just using his will power to make it happen. O.K.?

One . . .Two . . .Three . . .Go!!

Make sure the guy involved doesn't hold anything back. Have him give it every thing he's got and both of you put your entire attention on his progress.

Write down below, in detail, what happened.

"___________"

O.K.. Nothing happened, did it? In fact, the harder he tried and the more he put his attention on himself, the softer it got.

Benefits From Accepting Tumescence

If you accept the concept that women are the source of sexual arousal or turn on, you will find many benefits that come along with this idea.

One, is that if you are a man, you never have to worry about having an erection or maintaining one again. Whenever the woman in your life is turned on and really wants you, if you have enough attention on her, the little barometer between your legs will respond in a way that you cannot mistake.

Another benefit is that if you are a woman, this concept puts you in the driver's seat.

Couples who have worked with the idea that women are in charge have been pleased with the positive results in their sex life and relationship.

We will talk about Tumescence from this point on as a form of energy that is generated and transmitted by women. All that we ask is that you just keep an open mind and keep your eyes open.

Notes

Chapter Four

How Long Does It Take?

Once you have finished the book, answered the questions, and practiced the "Venus Butterfly" technique on yourself and each other once, you are already on your way.

The good news is also the bad news. You may never "master" the technique completely. There will always be more to learn. It is like golf or tennis. You can improve each time you practice and, like those popular sports, sex is more fun the better you get.

Regarding extending the length of your partner's orgasms, it really isn't important in itself. Of course, it is fun to measure your progress as you practice the techniques, but don't get caught up in accomplishing an ideal goal and dropping out the fun you could be having as you are improving.

More important than the number of orgasmic contractions your partner has is the intensity of those contractions. First focus on increasing the fun and pleasure you both are having. Once you relax and start having fun, the intensity and length of orgasmic contractions will increase on their own each time you make love.

Our most important advice is to take your time. Enjoy the journey. The most practical goal is to feel that you are increasing your sexual skills each time you make love, not to see how fast you can get there or how long you can make it last.

If you are still in a hurry, you will be excited to learn that we have made several "how-to" instructional videos and DVDs out of ***The One Hour Orgasm***.

The first is ***For His Eyes Only.*** The companion to this video/ DVD is called ***For Her Eyes Only.*** They not only *tell* you how to increase your and your partner's sexual pleasure, they *show* you as well.

Each describes in detail, and demonstrates, using attractive couples, the "Venus Butterfly" technique, and other ideas for enhancing and prolonging a romantic interlude. They can even help you instigate lovemaking when your partner isn't particularly in the mood. These videos are not pornographic. They are done tastefully; however, they contain nudity and are both very explicit (*so put the kids to bed before plugging them in*).

We highly recommend these videos and DVDs for a live demonstration of the "Venus Butterfly" technique. The videos and DVDs are produced by *The American Institute for Sexual Studies* and the information in this book have been featured on HBO, television shows, and radio talk shows all over the United States, Canada, and England. (See Recommended Books and Tapes at the end for more information.)

Why Resist More Pleasure In Your Life?

As you read *The One Hour Orgasm*, we recommended that you write out the answers to our questions as well as write down your thoughts, insights, and the feelings as you practice the "Venus Butterfly" technique.

As you already know, we have also provided fill-in-the-blank spaces so that you can easily respond to the questions as they are presented.

It is even a good idea to keep a separate, private, diary while you are reading and applying the techniques. Your diary is for your eyes only, unless you decide to share parts of it with your mate.

Notes

Chapter Five

Are You Normal?

Common Problems Which Show Up In Almost All Relationships

As you probably know, almost every couple runs into problems of some kind sooner or later in their relationship. See if any of these common issues affect you or your relationship in any way.

Please take a few minutes to take the following multiple choice test. If you are in a relationship, we have provided a test for you to take and one for your partner to take. You may also use it to analyze a past relationship.

Since some of your answers may concern or inhibit your partner, you may want to write your answers on a separate piece of paper or cut out the pages with your answers on them along the provided dotted line when you finish.

Questions For Her Eyes Only

1. Compared to the beginning of your relationship, the frequency of love making has:

a. Increased
b. Stayed the same
c. Decreased somewhat
d. Decreased a lot
e. Disappeared

2. Compared to the beginning of your relationship, the quality of love making has:

a. Gotten better
b. Stayed the same
c. Decreased somewhat
d. Decreased a lot
e. Disappeared

3. You have an orgasm when you make love:

a. Every time
b. Most of the time
c. 50% of the time
d. Seldom
e. Never.

4. He is sexually satisfied when you make love:

a. Every time
b. Most of the time
c. Seldom
d. Never.

5. Compared to the beginning of your relationship, your sex drive has:

a. increased
b. stayed the same
c. gone down a little
d. gone down significantly
e. disappeared

6. He reaches orgasm too quickly:

a. Most of the time
b. Often
c. Occasionally
d. Never.

7. You find that both of you are "in the mood" to make love:

a. Always at the same time
b. Mostly at the same time
c. Not usually at the same time
d. Never at the same time

8. You find that both of you have the energy at the same time to make love:

a. Always at the same time
b. Mostly at the same time
c. Not usually at the same time
d. Never at the same time

9. Usually, when just one of you wants to make love:

a. You make love
b. You make plans to make love
c. You make an excuse
d. He makes an excuse
e. You get into a fight

10. You use the excuse "not enough time" as a reason you don't make love more often:

a. Never
b. Sometimes
c. Often
d. Constantly

11. He uses "too tired" as a reason not to make love:

a. Never
b. Sometimes
c. Often
d. Constantly

12. You use "too tired" as a reason not to make love:

a. Never
b. Sometimes
c. Often
d. Constantly

13. He uses "I don't feel like it," or "I'm not in the mood," as a reason not to make love:

a. Never
b. Seldom
c. Often
d. Always

14. You use "I don't feel like it," or "I'm not in the mood," as a reason not to make love:

a. Never
b. Seldom
c. Often
d. Always

15. Some of the following items may affect your relationship one way or the other. Number them as to their importance to you, from 1 (least important) to 10 (most important):

__ Making money
__ Spending money
__ Saving money
__ Sex
__ Fun together
__ Fun apart
__ Work
__ Children
__ Television
__ Movies
__ Friends
__ Sports
__ Other ______________________________

16. Is sex becoming boring for him?

a. Yes
b. Maybe a little
c. No

17. Is sex becoming boring for you?

a. Yes
b. Maybe a little
c. No

18. Are you interested in learning how to sexually satisfy him more?

a. Yes
b. A little
c. No

19. Is he interested in being sexually satisfied more?

a. Yes
b. A little
c. No

20. Is he interested in learning how to sexually satisfy you more?

a. Yes
b. A little
c. No

21. Are you interested in being sexually satisfied more?

a. Yes
b. A little
c. No

22. Would he like for you to initiate love making more often than you presently do?

a. No
b. A little more often
c. A lot more often

23. Compared to the beginning of your relationship, he focuses on what he disapproves about you or what you do or don't do:

a. Less than in the beginning
b. Not at all
c. A little more
d. A lot more
e. All the time

24. Compared to the beginning of your relationship, you focus on what you disapprove about him or what he does or doesn't do:

a. Less than in the beginning
b. Not at all
c. A little more
d. A lot more
e. All the time

25. When you are not happy for any reason:

a. He is not happy
b. It affects him somewhat
c. It has no affect on him

26. When you say "No" to him about anything, for any reason, he honors your wishes:

a. Every time
b. Most of the time
c. Half the time
d. Not often
e. Never

27. When you want something (or when you want to do something) he listens to you, responds enthusiastically, and doesn't give you reasons why you can't have it:

a. Every time
b. Most of the time
c. Reluctantly
d. Not most of the time
e. Never

28. You give him a lot of praise when he does something for you:

a. Always
b. Very often
c. Half the time
d. Not very often
e. Never

29. You feel that he gives you a lot of praise when you do something for him and for your appearance:

a. Always
b. Very often
c. Half the time
d. Not very often
e. Never

30. He makes you more important than anything else in his life:

a. Always
b. Most of the time
c. Half the time
d. Not very often
e. Never

31. Do you think he should already know how to satisfy you sexually every time?

a. Yes
b. Somewhat
c. No

32. Does he think that he should already know how to satisfy you sexually every time?

a. Yes
b. Somewhat
c. No

33. Has either of your religious upbringings had an effect on your sex life?

a. A great deal
b. A notable influence

c. A little

d. Not at all

34. You set up sexually intimate and romantic "dates" with him (For our purposes, "dates" means setting aside and planning time together in order to be sexually intimate and romantic.):

a. Never

b. Rarely

c. I could do better

d. He is very satisfied with my efforts in this area

35. He sets up sexually intimate and romantic "dates" with you.

a. Never

b. Rarely

c. He could do better

d. I am very satisfied with his efforts in this area

36. You plan romantic dates together:

a. Rarely

b. Not at all

c. Not as many as we would like

d. We could do better

e. All the time

37. Compared to the beginning of your relationship, having "fun" together is an important priority for both of you:

a. Always

b. Most of the time

c. Half the time

d. Not as often as I would like

e. Not at all

38. Compared to the beginning of your relationship, how much has of the "spark" has gone out of your relationship:

a. None at all

b. A little of it

c. Most of it

d. All of it

39. Compared to the beginning of your relationship, How much of the "romance" has gone out of your relationship?

a. None at all
b. A little of it
c. Most of it
d. All of it

40. Does he agree and understand that if you, the woman he loves, are not happy, it will be impossible for him to be really happy?

a. No
b. A little
c. A great deal
d. Totally

41. Does he act as if he knows more about what feels good to you and how your body works than you do?

a. Yes
b. Often
c. Sometimes
d. Never

42. How often do you not feel good about your body and bring that feeling of unattractiveness into the bedroom with you?

a. Constantly
b. Much of the time
c. Half the time
d. Not often
e. Never

Questions For His Eyes Only

1. Compared to the beginning of your relationship, the frequency of love making has:

a. Increased
b. Stayed the same
c. Decreased somewhat
d. Decreased a lot
e. Disappeared

2. Compared to the beginning of your relationship, the quality of love making has:

a. Gotten better
b. Stayed the same
c. Decreased somewhat
d. Decreased a lot
e. Disappeared

3. As far as you know, she has an orgasm:

a. Every time
b. Most of the time
c. 50% of the time
d. Seldom
e. Never

4. You are sexually satisfied when you make love to her:

a. Every time
b. Most of the time
c. Seldom
d. Never

5. You have a problem getting turned on or maintaining an erection:

a. Most of the time
b. Often
c. Occasionally
d. Never

6. You feel that you reach orgasm too quickly:

a. Most of the time
b. Often
c. Occasionally
d. Never

7. You find that both of you are "in the mood" to make love:

a. Always at the same time
b. Mostly at the same time
c. Not usually at the same time
d. Never at the same time

8. You find that both of you have the energy at the same time to make love:

a. Always at the same time
b. Mostly at the same time
c. Not usually at the same time
d. Never at the same time

9. Usually, when just one of you wants to make love:

a. You make love
b. You make plans to make love
c. You make an excuse
d. She makes an excuse
e. You get into a fight

10. You use the excuse "not enough time" as a reason you don't make love more often:

a. Never
b. Sometimes
c. Often
d. Constantly

11. She uses "too tired" as a reason not to make love:

a. Never
b. Sometimes
c. Often
d. Constantly

12. You use "too tired" as a reason not to make love:

a. Never
b. Sometimes
c. Often
d. Constantly

13. She uses "I don't feel like it," or "I'm not in the mood," as a reason not to make love:

a. Never
b. Seldom
c. Often
d. Always

14. You use "I don't feel like it," or "I'm not in the mood," as a reason not to make love:

a. Never
b. Seldom
c. Often
d. Always

15. Some of the following items may affect your relationship one way or the other. Number them as to their importance to you, from 1 (least important) to 10 (most important):

__ Making money
__ Spending money
__ Saving money
__ Sex
__ Fun together
__ Fun apart
__ Work
__ Children
__ Television
__ Movies
__ Friends
__ Sports
__ Other ________________

16. Is sex becoming boring for her?

a. Yes
b. Maybe a little
c. No

17. Is sex becoming boring for you?

a. Yes
b. Maybe a little
c. No

18. Are you interested in learning how to sexually satisfy her more?

a. Yes
b. A little
c. No

19. Is she interested in being sexually satisfied more?

a. Yes
b. A little
c. No

20. Is she interested in learning how to sexually satisfy you more?

a. Yes
b. A little
c. No

21. Are you interested in her learning how to sexually satisfy you more?

a. Yes
b. A little
c. No

22. Would you like her to initiate love making more often than she presently does?

a. No
b. A little more often
c. A lot more often

23. Compared to the beginning of your relationship, she focuses on what she disapproves about you, or what you do or don't do:

a. Less than in the beginning
b. Not at all
c. A little more
d. A lot more
e. All the time

24. Compared to the beginning of your relationship, you focus on what you disapprove about her or what she does or doesn't do:

a. Less than in the beginning
b. Not at all
c. A little more
d. A lot more
e. All the time

25. When she is not happy for any reason:

a. You aren't happy
b. It affects you somewhat
c. It has no affect on you

26. If she says "no" about anything, for any reason, you honor her wishes:

a. Every time
b. Most of the time
c. Half the time
d. Not often
e. Never

27. When she wants something (or when she wants to do something) you listen to her, respond enthusiastically, and don't give her reasons why she can't have it:

a. Every time
b. Most of the time
c. Reluctantly
d. Not most of the time
e. Never.

28. You give her a lot of praise when she does something for you and for her appearance:

a. Always
b. Very frequently
c. Half the time
d. Not very often
e. Never

29. She gives you a lot of praise when you do something for her:

a. Always
b. Very frequently
c. Half the time
d. Not very often
e. Never

30. You make her more important than anything else in your life:

a. Always
b. Most of the time
c. Half the time
d. Not very often
e. Never

31. Does she act as if you should already know how to satisfy her sexually every time?

a. Yes
b. Somewhat
c. No

32. Do you think that you should already know how to satisfy her sexually every time?

a. Yes
b. Somewhat
c. No

33. Has either of your religious upbringings had an effect on your sex life?

a. A great deal

b. A notable influence
c. A little
d. Not at all

34. You set up sexually intimate and romantic "dates" with her (For our purposes, "dates" means setting aside and planning time together in order to be sexually intimate and romantic.):

a. Never
b. Rarely
c. I could do better
d. She is very satisfied with my efforts in this area

35. She sets up sexually intimate and romantic "dates" with you:

a. Never
b. Rarely
c. She could do better
d. I am very satisfied with her efforts in this area

36. You plan romantic dates together:

a. Rarely
b. Not at all
c. Not as many as we would like
d. We could do better
e. All the time

37. Compared to the beginning of your relationship, having "fun" together is an important priority for both of you:

a. Always
b. Most of the time
c. Half the time
d. Not as often as I would like
e. Not at all

38. Compared to the beginning of your relationship, how much has of the "spark" has gone out of your relationship:

a. None at all
b. A little of it

c. Most of it

d. All of it

39. Compared to the beginning of your relationship, How much of the "romance" has gone out of your relationship?

a. None at all

b. A little of it

c. Most of it

d. All of it

40. Do you agree and understand that if the woman you love is not happy, it will be impossible for you to be really happy?

a. No

b. A little

c. A great deal

d. Totally

41. Do you act as if you think that you know more about what feels good to her and how her body works than she does?

a. Yes

b. Often

c. Sometimes

d. Never

42. Do you think that if she doesn't feel good about the way her body looks, she brings that feeling of unattractiveness into the bedroom with her?

a. Constantly

b. Much of the time

c. Sometimes

d. Very seldom

e. Never

What's Next?

This may have been one of the toughest tests you have ever taken. Unlike some quizzes, this one has no bad or good score. The main purpose of these questions is to give you a starting place from which you might measure your progress over the next year.

The important issues are: What do you do with your findings? What are your choices? What will be the consequences of those choices?

Here is what we recommend: Wait until after you finish reading ***The One Hour Orgasm*** and have practiced the techniques on each other at least once before you talk about the results of the above quiz.

You may discover many of the solutions to your problems by then. The answers will come from improving your sexual skills and by learning how to have more fun and pleasure together, both in and out of the bedroom.

Setting Specific Common Goals

It is a good idea to use the personal information you discover from your answers to the above questions to come up with some specific goals, goals that you would like to achieve within a year or less of the day you finish ***The One Hour Orgasm***.

It is one thing to become aware of problems, differences of opinion and perception; however, it is another thing to know what to do about these issues. Just remember the old saying, "For every problem, there is an answer."

What if she thinks that the frequency of love making is too often and he thinks it is not often enough? Her goal could be to change the frequency to a level where she eagerly anticipates love making which is totally gratifying to her. His goal could be to change the frequency of love making so he does not feel deprived.

Resolving the above contradictory goals may seem hopeless at first; however, the principles in this book can be used to make sure that the needs of both partners are met.

What are your sexual and personal goals? If you could have every area of your relationship and sex life exactly the way you wanted it, what would you want to be different and how? Be as specific as you can.

Start by going back and circling at least 3 of the questions you answered that you would most like to see improvement in over the next year or less.

Next, go back to your circled items and set some specific goals, even if you do not know how you are going to accomplish them.

Be specific so that you can accurately measure your progress along the way. With each goal have a precise date and time by which you intend to achieve this improvement and include what the evidence will look like to prove that you have reached the goal.

Her Goals

____

____

____

____

____

His Goals

____

____

____

____

____

As you read through the book, follow the instructions, and add more goals, please come back to this part and write your new goals on this list. Writing your goals down as clearly as possible and referring to them often will help you crystallize the information you are receiving and speed up the results you will achieve.

Give Each Other A Break!

After taking the preceding test, please don't be hard on yourself (or your partner). Expecting to know how to satisfy a partner every time is unrealistic for most people until they learn to communicate effectively and improve their sexual skills.

Where did you or your partner get your sex education? Most of us get a large amount of our education and information about sex, not from our parents, but on the playground at school or on the street corner. This happens around the time we hit puberty. We are 9 to 12 years old or younger and our friends, who are the same age, fill us in.

We wind up with what we call a "Beavis and Butthead" sex education and vocabulary. Then we grow up and get married or get into a sexual relationship. Is it really a surprise, then, that many couples eventually have sexual and relationship problems?

What makes it worse is that, even after we become adults and get married, there is virtually no effective sex education available in America. It does not exist in our schools, churches, or the Yellow Pages.

To compound the problem, where effective sex education for adults is missing, pornography fills the void. Church and social leaders will often rail against lewd sexual material and abortion, but they almost never offer or endorse effective alternatives. The only guidance they offer regarding sex is negative or general and, worse yet, highly ineffective.

The solution lies in encouraging effective sex education for adults. We have seen some incredible results from working with adults who went home to put into practice what they have learned. You are now about to join their numbers.

Chapter Six

The Answer

A major complaint that marriage therapists hear today is that their patients "want to make love" but they "don't feel like it." They know they should make love more often, but the passionate force that was there in the beginning has disappeared.

What does it mean if your mate does not want to make love as much as when they were first married? Usually neither is involved with anyone else, and it is hard to understand why, after only a short number of years, one or both have become so disinterested.

All couples run into many of the same basic problems sooner or later. This book will provide the answers and information you have been looking for. Circle the following problem(s) you are most interested in solving:

1. The spontaneity has diminished or disappeared completely from your love making.

Impulsiveness goes away to some degree in every sexual relationship. This does not mean you are no longer in love. It is strong evidence that you are going to have to be more deliberate about your love making. In other words, make dates to be romantic and intimate, just as you did when you first met.

It is best that you first make and agree on a plan. What if you both enjoyed tennis? If you always waited until both of you just happened to have on your tennis clothes and you found yourselves standing on a tennis court, racquets in hand at the same time, with an hour or so and nothing better to do, tennis would not happen very often. Sex is no exception. Why should it be?

2. You are not in the mood, or lack the desire or energy, at the same time.

After the honeymoon period of the relationship, which usually lasts for 6 to 36 months, it is really very unrealistic to expect both of you to be in the mood and have the same amount of energy or desire at the same time. It is like expecting both of you to have an itch on your backs at the same time.

With the "Venus Butterfly" technique, you will never again have to wait around until your partner is in the mood. It only takes one of you to be in the mood for the technique to work. All your partner has to do is lie back and enjoy all of the pleasurable feelings which you will be creating for them.

If the lack of desire or energy comes up on either of your parts; just remember the official "Venus Butterfly" slogan:

"The Hungriest One Cooks!"

3. The frequency of your love making has gone down so much that one or both of you are feeling deprived.

Even if just one of you is feeling a little bit deprived, the situation is very dangerous and you should take steps to remedy it right away.

Using the "Venus Butterfly" technique, your frequency of love making will increase because your love making, sexual, sensual, and relationship skills will be improving. You will look forward to practicing the "Venus Butterfly" technique every time you don't have something better to do.

4. She isn't being satisfied romantically or physically.

Two out of every three American women don't have orgasms through intercourse whereas men generally do every time. This situation exists even though there is nothing wrong with the women or their bodies.

More University and The Institute of Human Abilities has not found one woman in over the last thirty years who cannot have orgasms if she wants to have them and is with a man who has practiced the "Venus Butterfly" technique.

We cannot entirely blame men for the the lack of female orgasm. Most men don't know how to satisfy the woman that they love every time. Most women we interviewed wished the man knew how to sexually please her without having to tell him.

5. One or both of you thinks or acts as if the man should already know everything about how to satisfy a woman every time.

Though very few men have been taught to be great lovers, most men assume they are. To make it worse, men often mistakenly think that if intercourse feels good to them, it must feel the same to the woman.

6. You have both stopped putting a priority on having fun together and being playmates.

Most of us start out as romantic playmates and then we get married or start living together. All of a sudden we become bill payers, home owners, career people, and parents. We can easily forget how important having fun together is to our relationship.

Practicing the "Venus Butterfly" technique gives you a great excuse to have more fun, be playmates again, regularly plan romantic and intimate dates, and practice and improve your skills in pleasuring each other.

7. You have stopped making it important to set aside specific times to go on intimate and romantic dates.

"Dating" or setting aside specific times to be alone, intimate, and romantic was one of the things you probably used to do at the beginning of your relationship. You were deliberate about spending time together. Now, it is if you both are waiting for the "Turn-On Fairy" to show up and, most likely, she hasn't been around for a long time.

8. The romance and intimacy has faded and gone away from your relationship.

Romance and intimacy decreases because you stop doing things which are romantic and intimate! Like a muscle that isn't exercised and shrinks. Your failure to revitalize your love making, diminishes it.

Even if love making is good for both of you, doing the same thing over and over won't continue working. We call this "coasting." In life, coasting takes you only in one direction...downhill.

9. She is one of the 81% of American women that, according to recent research, does not know how to or want to initiate love making in an effective way that is fun for both of you.

How is she supposed to know? Do you remember what they called girls in high school who liked or even talked about sex? Those were not flattering terms and being a "nice" girl did not get her the information or education she needed.

10. He acts as if he knows more about what feels good to her and about her body than she does.

Almost all women know that most men think this way. The big give-a-way is that men almost never ask questions. It is the same as when they get lost while driving. They won't pull over and ask for clear directions.

A sexually untrained man doesn't even know how to ask the right questions. If he gets lost in the bedroom, he just keeps driving until he runs out of gas or falls asleep.

11. He is one of the twenty to thirty million American men who suffer from the fear of impotency or premature ejaculation.

The good news is that impotency or premature ejaculation is not usually a physical problem. This is a popular myth that most men have been sold on and that the drug companies profit greatly from. Now we know for a fact that most impotency and premature ejaculation issues are not physical, but educational problems.

The main cause of impotency, that we have found, is that the man thinks that he causes his own erection. The harder he tries to have or maintain an erection and the more he worries about it, the worse matters get.

Premature ejaculation is also an educational problem. The victim of premature ejaculation has never learned how to control his levels of excitement, causing him to go over the top before his partner is ready.

12. He hasn't figured out yet that the woman he loves sets the ceiling on how happy he'll be.

How much evidence will he need to be convinced that if she is not happy, he cannot be truly happy? This is the hardest principle for some men to get, and yet the idea is so obvious. This insight is what makes it possible for both people in the relationship to feel like they are winning with each other both in and outside of the bedroom.

13. She doesn't feel good about her body and she continuously brings her doubt and that feeling of unattractiveness into the bedroom with her.

Women have a typical way of looking at themselves in the mirror which is strange to men.

> **Women look in the mirror for what is wrong with them.**

And worse, next, she makes sure that she calls her husband over and says, "Look how fat I'm getting. Look at this cellulite! Look at these wrinkles and flab. How can you stand to even look at me? I hate my body!"

The man is astonished. "Gee baby, I think you look wonderful.," he says.

"Shut up!" she fires back. "I'm fat and I look disgusting!"

The sad ending to this story is that after years and years of this interchange, one day she *finally* enrolls him into how unattractive she looks and then wonders why he isn't turned on by her anymore.

Practicing the principles in *The One Hour Orgasm,* both partners will learn how to focus on what they find attractive about each other. The more they practice this approach, the more things they will find to approve of and get turned on about.

You will discover that the more you verbally appreciate and approve of your partner, the more they will want to please you and make you happy.

14. She seldom or never thanks him for everything he does and repeatedly complains about everything that makes her unhappy.

The biggest complaint we hear from men is, "I do ninety-nine things right and never hear a word about it. I do one thing wrong and she never lets me hear the end of it!"

15. He seldom or never appreciates her, values her, shows her that he loves her, or thanks her for all the things that she does. He may repeatedly complain about everything that he disapproves of regarding her or her actions.

The same issue is being triggered in the above two problems which is...

> **In life you always get more of what you focus on. If you go out into the garden and water only the weeds, you're going to wind up with more weeds.**

16. She doesn't give him information about her body and expects him to be a mind reader.

Maybe she doesn't know a lot about her own body or if she does, she doesn't want to hurt his feelings. It is much easier for most women to say, "Would you please pass the salt," than it is for them to ask, "Would you please move a quarter of an inch to the left."

17. He puts his job, watching sports, being with his friends, or his goals ahead of her pleasure.

Most women hate to play second fiddle to anyone or any of his goals. She expects to be the most important thing in his life.

18. She gets angry with him.

In over 30 years of research, only one main reason could be found for why women get angry…they are not getting what they want.

Anger and love cannot exist at the same time, and anger is always destructive. Anger hurts both people. He may suffer, but her anger will also slow down the delivery of her true goals.

The good news is that: The techniques and the philosophy in ***The One Hour Orgasm*** and in its companion videos, ***For His Eyes Only…How To Make Sex More Fun For Her***, ***For Her Eyes Only…How To Make Sex More Fun For Him***, and ***The Ultimate Guide To Making A Relationship Work***, will help reduce many of these anger related problems.

This "Venus Butterfly" technique will put the total control to pleasure or be pleasured in your hands. You will want to "do it" because you will know that every moment is going to be pleasurable, and the "Venus Butterfly" communication techniques will guarantee that your love making will continue to get better and better because you will always know exactly what you are doing.

Chapter Seven

The Famous "Venus Butterfly" Technique

Would you really like to know how to be satisfied or to satisfy your partner every time? Does the idea of increasing the intensity and duration of your sexual encounters motivate you?

Are you ready to begin to feel the limitless pleasure that you suspect will be there for you and your mate?

A common answer is: "Not necessarily."

There are a lot of reasons to procrastinate, to find other things to do, and reasons not to follow the instructions we are about to give you.

The desire not to be vulnerable, the possibility of failure, and other fears may come up for you. It is natural that you may want to delay because of a sudden desire for food or a nap. Even thoughts such as "I don't want to," "I'm too tired," "I haven't got the time," and small emergencies, etc.

It is perfectly normal for you to have those feelings and think those thoughts. Don't worry. Just know that what you are feeling is normal resistance and go ahead and follow the instructions. This moment is an excellent opportunity to have a breakthrough and to notice how you may tend to both consciously and unconsciously resist pleasure in your life.

If you still feel like you are in the molasses of procrastination, don't fight it. Just go into slow motion. Slow down and do only one...sentence...at...a...time.

Get a sense that you are winning by moving forward, but don't stop. Slow down until the feeling of resistance passes.

Lighten up! Stop taking your "thoughts" so seriously and have some fun with your resistance. Defy your mind's delaying tactics, and do the next sexercise anyway.

Shopping List

To begin learning how to master the "Venus Butterfly" technique and produce longer and more intense orgasms, the first things you need are the following supplies and equipment. Round them up from around the house or make a list right away so that you can borrow or go shopping for the missing items as soon as possible.

1. A large hand mirror. Not a compact mirror. It must be at least as large as your outstretched hand.

2. A full-length mirror. Buy a five-foot mirror if you do not already have one. Mount it on the door or on a sturdy stand.

3. A jar or tube of lubricant. Get the brand *Vaseline*™ for this experience. You may eventually switch to another brand or use a water-based lubricant, but More University feels that it is important that you start with Vaseline for the following "sexercise."*

*Vaseline is not water soluble, so not even perspiration will wash it off. It also spreads and *radiates* pleasurable sensations. Vaseline seems to have a preferable consistency even though it is made of basically the same ingredients as other brands.

4. Body lotion or massage oil.

5. As many items as possible to please your eyes such as candles or flowers.

6. Something to please your nose: scented bath oil, your favorite perfume or cologne, flowers, incense, or scented candles.

7. Something to please your ears: romantic music…a tape player with or without earphones, a blank cassette tape to record the instruction on (optional), and a CD or cassette tape of your favorite romantic music or at least a radio tuned to a romantic music station.

8. Something to give pleasure to your taste buds…something wonderful to eat or drink. At least one of your simple most favorite foods or drinks, such as your favorite kind of chocolate or a glass of champagne or freshly squeezed orange juice.

9. A private space where you can have all of the above assembled for at least one and one-half hours without interruption. You may wish to borrow a friend's place or even consider renting a hotel room. Make sure you have access to a bathtub or shower.

10. A flashlight.

11. This book and a pen.

Ready? Get Set! Go!

There are five parts to this "sexercise."

Complete one before you go on to the other. You will only know how important it is to do all parts of this sexercise after you have completed all the steps.

Until you are finished, just take our word that doing this sexercise will make all the difference in the world to your future sex life.

The two most important ingredients are: your willingness to do the exercise to the best of your ability, and…***doing it***.

You are about to take the single biggest step you have probably ever taken in order to learn how to satisfy your partner, be satisfied by your partner, and to train your nervous system to have orgasms which can be more intense and last up to one hour.

You may exercise regularly to stay in shape and to keep yourself healthy. You may even work out with weights to keep your body hard and fit. We are recommending that you work out your sexual nervous system so that it can work better for you.

Warning: Merely reading about the sexercises in this book will do you about as much good as reading about someone going to a gym and working out.

If you do the following sexercise from the More University Basic Sensuality Course even just once a week, you will be able to have more fun and pleasure than you could otherwise imagine.

If you don't do the sexercises, you won't get the results which thousands of people have achieved before you. And, please…do the following basic "Venus Butterfly" sexercises at least one time before you do the "Venus Butterfly" technique with your partner.

Congratulations. You are on your way to having the best sex life you can imagine.

This first step takes only thirty minutes after you read through all of the instructions. You could spends hours just to complete the next step, *but do not spend more than thirty minutes*. Taking too much time during this step will diminish your success. It may even be an unconscious attempt to resist creating more pleasure.

The "Visiting Movie Star"

Dr. Victor Baranco called this the "Visiting Dignitary" part of the Basic Sensuality course taught at More University and The Institute Of Human Abilities for over the last 30 years.

Pretend that a very important person has requested to use a room in your home. Imagine that it is someone very special. Maybe your favorite movie star, world leader, or visiting royalty.

What do you do?

Begin now to make the room as nice as you can. Throw any clutter in a closet or out of sight, and make sure there are as many visually attractive items to look at as you can arrange.

Checklist

❍ Set out some scented candles (you'll light them later).

❍ Set flowers out where they can be visually enjoyed from anywhere in the room.

❍ Have your favorite romantic music set up and playing softly so that the visitor's ears will experience pleasure.

❍ Set out some of your favorite perfume or cologne available so your guest can dash some lightly on his or her body. Also have ready your body lotion or massage oil and Vaseline.

❍ Prepare some of your favorite foods or drinks, so you can bring it out at the appropriate time.

❍ Make sure the bathroom is clean, and arrange it so that your guest can take a bubble bath or shower. Set out the best soap and fragrances you have.

Important: Stop getting the room ready as soon as your thirty minutes are up.

The One Hour Orgasm

Change In Plans

After everything has been set up, imagine that the phone rings and your movie star, world leader, or royalty has had to postpone the visit.

Well, no use letting all these preparations go to waste. You will use this wonderful space to do your basic "Venus Butterfly" sensuality sexercises.

Ready?

Taking A Sensual Bath

The purpose of taking this bath, which should take no more than 15 minutes, is to begin to wash away the tensions of the day and open your body up to feelings of pleasure.

Checklist

❍ Go to the bathroom and set out your candles and sweet fragrances such as perfume, cologne, bubble bath, and bath oils.

❍ Draw your bath with just the temperature and fragrance you want.

❍ Undress, hanging or folding your clothes nicely and neatly as if it were for someone for whom you cared a great deal.

❍ Once you are undressed, slowly let yourself down into the bath water. Savor how the water feels as it touches each part of your body.

Splash the water on different parts to see how good the water feels to your skin.

What parts of you are enjoying the bath the most? Can you do something to allow the other parts of your body to also enjoy the feel of the water?

How much can you let yourself experience the light from the candles and the sweet fragrances?

❍ When your fifteen minutes are up, get out of the bath, slowly and gently dry yourself off.

Jot down anything that you found pleasurable about the experience you just had:

____

____

____

____

____

If you surprised your mate with the sensual bath you just experienced, what do you imagine their reaction would be?

____

____

____

____

____

Finding Things To Like About Your Body

This next part of the sexercise is *very* important. It may help you to use a tape recorder. If you do, first record all of the following instructions, step by step. Then play them back to yourself as you are going through the sexercises. You may find it easier to turn the tape recorder on and off, instead of going back and forth to the book.

Ready?

Make sure the place you are using is warm enough for you to be nude for about one hour.

The One Hour Orgasm

Avoid the tendency to skip over or rush through any of the following steps.

1. With all your clothes off, get your hand mirror and go over to your full length mirror. Go over every inch of your body and find every area about which you can *find something to like*.

Normally, your attention tends only to be on the bad parts. You may keep saying and demonstrating that you are disappointed in your body. Remember, every time you do this, you are "watering the weeds."

Have a breakthrough. Cross the line over to being a person committed to more fun and pleasure; look only and specifically for things you like about your body.

If you come across an area you can find absolutely nothing good about, despite your best efforts, pass by it quickly and let go of that judgment. Just go on to the next area.

2. Start with the top of your head.

❍ Look at the top of your head. You will need both mirrors to do this properly. Hold the smaller mirror over your head and tilt it so that you can see the top of your head in the full-length mirror.

Talk to yourself as if you were talking to another person, describing the good and interesting things that you see during the following exploration of your body. When you come to any part of your body that is a working or movable part, see how it looks and feels to squeeze it and wiggle and move it around.

❍ What different shades of colors do you notice about each area on your body? What different shapes can you make out?

❍ Closely examine your ears, wiggle them around with your fingers. What do you notice?

❍ Which direction does your hair grow on different parts of your body.

As you lightly touch your body hair and notice that, like a cat's whiskers, you can pick up sensory input with it. This information will come in handy the next time you are making love to your partner.

❍ Lightly and lovingly touch the hair on your eyebrows and eyelids. How does that feel?

❍ Look closely at the skin on your face and neck. Can you see the different colors and types of skin in each area?

❍ Check both eyes. Are they exactly the same? If not, describe the differences.

❍ Look at your lips. Is the skin inside your mouth like the skin on your lips? Describe the differences you see.

3. Here's something you have never done before. Have you ever looked at your rectum in your whole life? If you're like most people, you don't even want to know what it looks like. Almost everybody imagines that it's horrible and disgusting. Look at it anyway.

❍ Place your hand-held mirror on the floor. Get your flashlight. Squat down over the mirror. Shine the light into the mirror to illuminate your rectum, and see what it looks like. Describe anything attractive you can find about it.

Thoroughly examine your sexual organs.

❍ If you are a woman, look at the outer lips of your vagina. Can you see that it looks somewhat like a flower? Do you see the petals?

❍ If you are a man, closely examine your scrotum and penis from below. Can you see the variations of color, the different types of skin tissue, and the different kinds of hair growth?

4. Now, starting with the bottom of your feet, look at every part of your body that you have not examined yet. Remember, you are looking for things to like. Be aware and interested in the variations of color and the different types of skin tissue on every part of your body . Use both mirrors when necessary to see yourself from every angle. *Don't forget your back.*

❍ Describe the variations of color and the different types of skin tissue that you see.

After doing all of the above, do you still believe you really need to be as embarrassed or ashamed as you were about many of your body parts?

__No

__Much less

__Yes

__Much more

What, if anything, about your former beliefs, has changed?

__Nothing

__A little

__A lot

Comments____

____

____

____

____

5. Using the full-length mirror, try a few different poses and positions that make you look the most attractive.

Like most humans, you probably were not very proud of certain parts of your body. Many people cannot quickly think of even one thing they like about their bodies.

Have you ever stood in front of a mirror saying derogatory things about yourself? "Look at those fat thighs! What an ugly body! Look at that flabby skin. How could anyone who looks like this ever show themselves in public?"

If you don't think that saying things like that to yourself is cruel and abusive, try this: Go to one of your favorite restaurants and stand outside. As people come out, point at them and say the same things to them as you do to yourself. "Look at those fat thighs!" and so on.

If you followed these instructions, it wouldn't take you long to recognize how abusive this sort of behavior is and how bad you have been to yourself, would it?

This behavior is called "beating yourself up." The point is that beating yourself up isn't constructive behavior. It doesn't work. You don't get better. It is that same kind of behavior as going out to your garden every day and only watering the weeds.

Anything, positive or negative, that you give your attention to expands. Why give attention any longer to the negative things? You have two choices. Get into immediate action and do something to fix them or learn to love them.

Had Any Breakthroughs Yet?

You may have already made one important observation. If you did this part of your sexercise properly, you looked for what you liked about your body.

How is looking for what is good about your body different than what you usually do?

__It's totally different

__It's a little different

__There's no difference

Comments____

____

____

____

____

Up until now, have you usually looked for what was wrong, beat yourself up, or blanked out parts of your body?

__Yes

__Somewhat

__No

Comments____

____

____

____

____

What is the result, in the past, when you have only looked for what is wrong with your body?

__I feel worse

__I feel better

__There's no change

Comments____

____

____

____

____

What do you suppose you get out of looking only for the bad?

__It inspires me to get into action

__It helps me to accept myself

__Other ____________________________

What did you discover by looking just for what is good about your body?

__I was more confident

__I was less confident

__Nothing happened

__Other ____________________________

Will you be able to enjoy your own body more after this exercise, rather than automatically checking for what is wrong?

__Yes

__Maybe

__No

If so, what specifically could you do that would be different?

____

____

____

____

____

Will you now be able to enjoy in your partner's body more after this exercise?

__Yes

__A little more

__No

If so, what specifically might you do that is different?

____

____

____

____

____

Which of the following do you do most often:

__Looking only for the bad when you look at your body?

__Looking only for the bad when you look at your partner's body?

__Looking only for the good when you look at your body?

__Looking only for the good when you look at your partner's body?

Which of the following would you actually find more pleasurable:

__Looking only for the bad when you look at your body?

__Looking only for the bad when you look at your partner's body?

__Looking only for the good when you look at your body?

__Looking only for the good when you look at your partner's body?

Reality Check

According to a recent study, only one out of every ten people will admit to being at their ideal weight. They don't like at least some part of their body.

It is a miracle, isn't it, that very many of us have the nerve to take our clothes off and let another person see us? The amount of negative perceptions most of us have about our bodies, as Mr. Spock would say, "seems illogical."

Tactile Inventory

On this next 15-minute part of your sexercise you may also want to start out by recording the following instructions so that you can play them back to yourself.

Get Started

❍ Get out a jar of Vaseline and a large towel or sheet.

❍ Put the towel or sheet over the bed or place where you are going to sit or lie down.

❍ Pinch the skin over your elbow as hard as you can.

Do you notice how insensitive the elbow area is? Not much feeling, is there?

❍ Now pinch with equal pressure the skin on the inside of your elbow.

Notice how your sensing ability varies from one area to the other.

The "Venus Butterfly" "Taking" Touch

When you touch velvet, does the velvet feel good or does your hand? Your hand does, of course. Touching velvet is an example of what we call a "Taking Touch." Intend to "take" pleasure when you are touching yourself or later when you are touching your partner.

You need not be concerned about "giving" pleasure to your partner. When you are aware of "taking" pleasure with your touches, you feel pleasure which is almost as good as being touched. You will begin to discover that what feels best to you will probably feel good to your partner.

Circles

❍ Next, with your fingers, start making large circles on the inside of your forearm.

What is the speed and pressure that feels the best, both to your fingers and also to your skin?

__I like it slow
__I like it fast
__I like light pressure
__I like heavy pressure

If you wish, describe your findings below.

____

____

____

____

____

Fingernails

❍ Now, touch your skin with the edge and even the backs of your fingernails.

❍ Also, try touching yourself lovingly with just the hairs on your hand.

Can you "take" pleasuring sensations with just your nails?

Does your skin like receiving touch this way?

__Yes
__A little
__No

Lubricant

Now, see what it feels like to use a little lubricant.

❍ Get a very small amount of Vaseline and warm it up by rubbing a small amount in your hands.

❍ Apply it to the inside of your forearm, using small circular movements.

Compare how different this feels than it did when you were rubbing "dry," without lubricant. Do you notice that using the lubricant causes the sensations to spread like the ripples in a pond when a pebble hits the water?

❍ Next, begin to explore both sides of your upper and lower arm using the same small circular movements.

❍ Lightly touch the hair to see how that feels.

❍ Do the same to your hands and fingers,

❍ Your shoulders,

❍ Both sides of your neck,

❍ All parts of your face,

❍ Around your eyes,

❍ Each part of your ears,

❍ And, especially your upper lip.

Notice if there is a difference between rubbing your lower lip and upper lip.

Which lip is most sensitive?

__Upper
__Lower

Does the inside or the outside of your lip, have more feeling?

__Inside
__Outside

When you touch your lips, if you try, can you feel pleasant sensations in your genital area? ____Yes ____No

❍ Move on to your chest, using small circular movements.

❍ Gently explore your nipples,

❍ Your stomach,

❍ The trunk of your body,

❍ The sides of your legs,

❍ The tops and bottoms of your feet,

❍ Your toes.

Pay special attention to your middle toe. Many people report that they have been able to develop pleasant sexual feelings, even orgasmic genital contractions, from rubbing with the "taking" touch.

Men: At this point, skip past the **Sexercises For Women Only** section to the section marked **Sexercises For Men Only**. (Don't worry. You won't miss anything. Later, you will be instructed to come back and read this section.)

Sexercises For Women Only

The genital area will be the most sensitive of your body because of the high number of nerve endings located there.

❍ Start exploring by slowly stroking the lower part of your stomach and then, as if you were slowly drawing a big circle, let your hand slowly glide down the top part of your thigh, crossing over just underneath the genital area without touching your pubic hair, slowly up your other thigh, and then back up to your stomach.

❍ Very slowly make the circle smaller and smaller until you begin to barely feel your pubic hairs.

❍ Gently begin to lightly stroke the hairs with your fingers and both sides of your hand.

Remember to continue to use "taking" touches.

The Famous "Venus Butterfly" Technique

❍ Next, using your mirror to see the area you are touching, gently apply Vaseline to the outer lips of your vagina.

❍ Slowly work in toward the inner lips. Notice which particular places are the most sensitive.

❍ Rub the opening area of your vagina (the entrance).

❍ Also gently rub on the outside of the hole to the urethra, which is your urinary opening.

❍ Feel inside the opening of your vagina.

❍ Make sure you have plenty of Vaseline on your fingers and with one or two fingers, reach as far inside the vaginal canal as you can.

❍ Press against the vaginal wall with increasing pressure.

Start with very light pressure at first and then find out how much pressure you can apply without feeling any pain.

❍ Try pushing at 6 o'clock, that is toward the floor.

❍ Then at the 3 o'clock area.

❍ And 9 o'clock.

❍ Last, push and rub against the upper part or 12 o'clock and feel for a rough round spot about the size of a nickel.

When you press against this last position, you may be able to feel stimulation as if you were pushing against the back of your clitoris.

This is the famous "G-Spot" area and it may feel uncomfortable to your touch except when you are very excited and turned on such as just prior to and during an orgasm.

The Love Button

❍ Now, begin to explore your clitoris. Make sure you have plenty of warm lubricant on your fingers.

❍ Feel the hood that covers the clitoris. This piece of skin is like the foreskin on a man before he is circumcised.

Do not try to cause an orgasm while you are doing this sexercise. If you become too excited, stop or slow down until you regain control.

❍ Pull the hood back and rub on the clitoris.

❍ Explore all sides of your clitoris, especially just underneath the hood.

Discover the Most Sensitive Part of the Clitoris

For most women your upper left side (at 1 o'clock from the man's point of view...11 o'clock from your point of view when looking into your mirror) will be the most sensitive.

Which is the most sensitive part of your clitoris at this time?

____

____

____

____

Which part do you favor when you are masturbating?

____

____

____

____

____

You might have developed the sensitivity of another part of your clitoris by favoring it during masturbation; however, if you will include and stimulate the 1 o'clock part, it will soon become your favorite and most sensitive spot.

When you are feeling for this 1 o'clock area, try rubbing slowly with a lot of lubricant on your finger right under the hood at 1 o'clock. You should be able to feel a little groove or ridge there under the hood. That's the spot.

❍ Last, begin to explore the area around your second most sensitive area, your anus. There are many nerve endings close to this area. Again, make sure you are using a lubricant while you are exploring this area.

If you are a little timid about exploring your anus, you may be more comfortable using a latex examination glove to cover your whole hand or a latex finger cover or condom to cover your exploring finger. If you use latex, coat the outside of the latex with a water based lubricant before you begin to explore. It usually is not a good idea to use Vaseline. Vaseline will melt latex in a very short period of time; however, for the brief time you will be exploring, the latex should hold up.

After you have completed this part of the sexercise, throw away the latex protection, if any was used, and go wash the remaining lubricant off your hands and get ready for the next part.

For now, skip past the **Sexercises For Men Only** section to the **Stimulation For Pleasurable Effect** section on page 76.

Sexercises For Men Only

The genital area will be the most sensitive part of your body because of the high number of nerve endings located there.

❍ Start by touching the lower part of your stomach and then, as if you were slowly drawing a big circle, let your hand slowly glide down the top part of your thigh, crossing over just underneath the genital area without touching your genitals, slowly up your other thigh, and then back up to your stomach.

❍ Very slowly make the circle smaller and smaller until you begin to barely feel your pubic hairs and genitals.

❍ Gently begin to lightly stroke the hairs with your fingers and both sides of your hand. Remember to continue to use "taking" touches.

❍ Next, take a liberal amount of Vaseline and rub it between your hands to warm it.

❍ Gently and slowly begin to apply the Vaseline to your penis and scrotum, the sack that surrounds your testicles.

❍ Begin to feel the different parts of your penis. Start with the urethra opening, the hole at the end of your penis.

❍ Next, gently and slowly, with "taking" touches, explore the crown, which is the area around the hole, and work down to the ridge of the crown. This is called the coronal ridge.

Notice where you have the most pleasurable sensations.

See if there is more feeling on one side of your penis than the other, or in one spot versus another.

Do not try to cause an orgasm while you are doing this sexercise. If you become too excited, stop or slow down until you regain control.

❍ Next, move slowly down to the shaft of the penis.

See if you can tell that the sides and top of the shaft have less feeling than the underside part of the shaft.

Does the upper part of your penis, toward the crown, have more feeling than the lower part? ____Yes ____No

❍ Grasp the base of the shaft of the penis by wrapping your thumb and forefinger around it and press down.

❍ Next, wrap the thumb and forefinger of your other hand around the top of the sack of your testicles.

❍ Now, very slowly pull down with increasing pressure and see how much pressure your testicles can take.

Are you surprised at how much pressure you can take?

❍ With your lower hand, surround your testicles and slowly begin to squeeze them in a downward motion. Increase the pressure slowly until you feel discomfort or until you can squeeze no harder, whichever comes first.

❍ Last, put some more Vaseline on your fingers and lubricate the area around your anus.

❍ Explore this area with your fingers and notice the areas which are the most sensitive.

If you are a little timid about exploring your anus, you may be more comfortable using a latex examination glove to cover your whole hand or a latex finger cover or condom to cover your exploring finger. If you use latex, coat the outside of the latex with a water based lubricant before you begin to explore. It is usually not a good idea to use Vaseline. Vaseline will melt latex in a very short period of time, however, for the brief time you will be exploring, the latex should hold up.

❍ Before you stop, press in and stoke back and forth, with increasing pressure, on the area between your anus and the sack of your scrotum. This is a man's "G Spot." Your prostate lies buried inside this area and it is sensitive to pleasurable sensations when you are aroused.

It may not feel tremendously pleasurable to press and rub on this area except when you are very excited and turned on such as just prior to and during an orgasm.

After you have finished this part of the sexercise, throw away the latex protection, if any was used, wash the remaining lubricant off your hands, and get ready for the remaining sexercises.

Stimulation For Pleasurable Effect

It makes sense that if you know the very best way to touch yourself, you will better know how to tell your partner what feels best to you. You will also benefit by getting a better understanding about what will feel best when you touch your partner.

> **"You have to know what you want, before you can tell anyone else what you want."**

Achieving orgasm is not the purpose of this sexercise. Your goal is to feel as good as possible for as long as possible. Orgasm should be avoided at this particular time to get the most value.

Do this sexercise by yourself.

Read all of the instructions before you begin. Either lay the book out so that you can refer to the instructions as you go along or record them on your tape recorder and play them back to yourself as you are doing the sexercises.

❍ Set out your Vaseline. You will need it for lubrication from time to time in this process.

❍ Make sure your towel is handy.

❍ Light your candles.

❍ Turn on your favorite romantic music.

❍ Bring out the special food or drink you prepared earlier.

What you will be doing is a sexercise in tumescence: to begin to play with the sexual energy in your body, to increase and decrease sexual tension at your command.

Relax and enjoy the sexercise. There is no pressure on you to perform sexually or accomplish a result. Pleasure is your only goal.

Warm up some massage oil or body lotion in your hands and begin by slowly and sensually stroking places on your body that may not have received much attention for a long time. Begin at the top of your head and work down to your genitals. Then start at your feet and work up. Don't include your genitals as yet…you'll get to them later.

Go slow and take your time. Get as much pleasurable sensation out of each place as you can before going onto the next part of your body.

Try out different kinds of pressure from very light to heavy on each area. At the same time, try different speeds from very slow to fast to see which feels the best to you.

Sexual Teasing

"Teasing" is causing a feeling of scarcity in one place by creating an abundance of feeling in another.

Start on the outside, the outer perimeter, of your nipples. With your fingers, slowly make large circles around this area, and gradually move in toward the center using smaller and smaller circles.

Imagine that you are creating an "itch" that wants to be scratched. When the place you are teasing begins to anticipate that you are about to touch it, tease it some more by waiting a little longer.

Now—when you are good and ready—sensually touch the area you have been teasing.

The One Hour Orgasm

Notice that you have the power to create some interesting effects even when experimenting on your own body. (Later, you will be able to cause the same sensations when you are pleasuring your partner's body.)

Men: For now, skip past the **More Sexercises For Women Only** section and proceed to the **More Sexercises For Men Only** section on page 82.

More Sexercises For Women Only

Wipe the massage oil off your hands with your towel. Scoop out a liberal amount of Vaseline and warm it by rubbing it between your fingers.

Begin to slowly and gently spread it on:

1. the outer lips of her vagina (labia majora),

2. then her inner lips (labia minora),

3. then the opening to her vagina (not up inside, just on the opening).

4. Finally, follow the inner lips up to the point that they begin to form the hood over the clitoris. Carefully and slowly lubricate the hood of the clitoris and very gently include the head of the clitoris (clitoral glans) itself.

As you are applying lubricant, spread your fingers and toes to feel sensations throughout your whole body. Most women report that when they do this, they experience more intense sensations.

Use a lot of Vaseline. Vaseline spreads sensation and prevents skin irritation. It also allows you to easily use both heavy or light pressure.

5. Begin to stroke your clitoris slowly and gently. Which part of your clitoris feels the best when you touch or stroke it?

Experiment with different pressures and speeds to determine which feels best to you. There is no hurry. Take your time. Notice that the more tumesced or excited you become, the more pressure you can enjoy.

Which pressure feels best to you? Light? Heavy? In between?

Which speed feels best to you? Very slow? Fast? In between?

Peaking

"Peaking" is a technique that is designed to increase your ability to feel more than you presently do.

As you continue the sexercise and your tumescence builds, bring yourself as close to the upper side of that feeling as is possible without going over the top…then let yourself down and regain control by trying one of the following methods: Stopping…Slowing down…Changing to a lighter pressure, or...Changing the direction you are rubbing.

Notice that each time you build up to the edge, the intensity of the feeling increases. If you continue to do this, you will be able to build the intensity to the highest point possible.

On a graph, peaking would look like this:

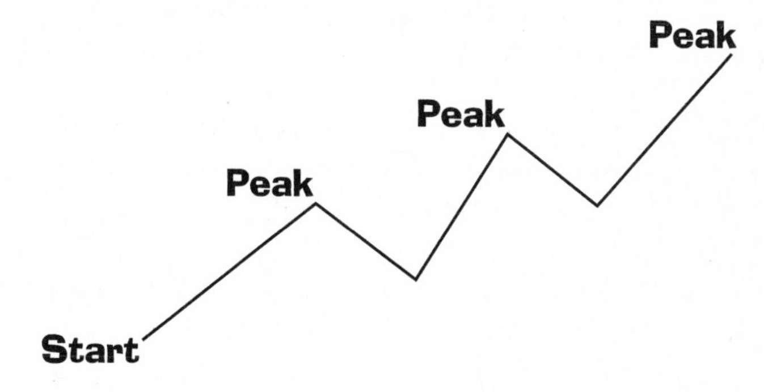

Notice that on the graph, the peaks keep going up to higher levels. Without "Peaking" you could not get to those levels.

Keep "Peaking" yourself as long as it is pleasurable to you. Remember, your goal right now is to feel as good as possible for as long as possible.

Important: Do not go over the top while doing this sexercise. If you become too excited...stop until you regain control.

Right now, you are going for the longest and most pleasurable effect, not an orgasm.

An orgasm causes the release of built-up sexual energy or tumescence. The more you put into the "peaking" of your orgasm, the more sexual energy or tumescence you will release. Your orgasmic contractions will last longer and be stronger than they have ever been before.

Connecting

"Connecting" is sexual stimulation without direct genital contact. It's learning to feel pleasure in the genital area when being kissed or touched in other (secondary) places of your body such as your lips, neck, or ears.

Once you get an area turned on and connected, you can bring yourself or your partner to at least the edge of an orgasm using only the secondary area.

You can "connect" any two areas of your body or your partner's body using the following technique.

❍ Lightly apply warmed Vaseline to another place on your body. Start with your facial lips.

❍ Continue to rub on your clitoris and at the same time begin to "tease" your facial lips by slowly stroking the outside edges using wide circles.

❍ Let your fingers move gradually toward your facial lips. Once you begin touching them, they should be very excited and turned on.

❍ At the same time, rub your clitoris with the *same* pressure and movement you are using on your lips. See if you can duplicate the feelings you are having in one area in the other.

❍ Take your hand off your clitoris and see if it can feel any of the sensations you are creating in your lips.

❍ After a while, begin to rub on your clitoris again using the same pressure and movement as you are using on your lips.

❍ Now, take your hand off your lips and see if they can feel any of the sensations you are creating in your clitoris.

Keep switching back and forth until you feel you have gone as far as you can for now.

Do this "connecting" exercise using as many parts of your body as is pleasurable for you.

Try the following areas and write down between 1 (low sensations) to 10 (extremely high sensations) the response you are able to create between the parts you are using. Once you get an area turned on and connected, see if you can bring yourself to the edge of an orgasm using only the secondary area.

❍ The middle toe of your left or right foot ____

❍ Just your upper lip ____

❍ Your ear lobe ____

❍ The inside of your elbow ____

❍ The inside of your thigh ____

❍ Your nipples ____

❍ The outer part of your vaginal opening ____

❍ The inside of your vaginal canal ____

❍ Your "G" spot ____

❍ and also the arch of your foot ____

Do this sexercise as long as it feels good, continuing to "peak" yourself until the pleasurable feelings you were having are starting to go down or even bottom out.

At any time that you stop having good feelings from rubbing yourself…stop! Just say out loud to yourself, ***"This concludes the sexercise."***

If you go too far and cannot stop yourself from having an orgasm during the exercise, before you orgasm say out loud, ***"This concludes the sexercise."***

What is the level of your sexual tension or tumescence? High? Low? Totally flat?

When you are ready, wash the lubricant off your hands, take a few moments to lie still and be aware of how each part of your body is feeling.

Women: For now, skip past the **More Sexercises For Men Only** section and proceed to **Chapter 8** on page 89.

Wipe the massage oil off your hands with your towel. Next, take a liberal amount of Vaseline and rub it between your hands to warm it up.

Apply the Vaseline to your penis and scrotum.

It's unlikely that you will have an erection at this point, but it doesn't matter. Regardless, start with the following approach.

❍ Make a circle with the thumb and index finger of each of your hands.

❍ Encircle the shaft of your penis at its base with your left hand.

❍ Holding your left hand firmly at the base of your penis, gently and slowly slide your right hand, using only your thumb and index finger, up the shaft, stretching the penis gently until you reach the top. Apply more pressure at the bottom and lighten up as you near the top. This gentle motion will not only feel good to you, it also draws blood into the penis, making it harder and more erect.

You will find the above method valuable in persuading your penis to respond any time you want it to, or if you want to harden an already full erection.

❍ As your penis enlarges, you can use more than two fingers to form your "rings." Continue to do this until your penis becomes erect.

The Pause That Refreshes

If your penis is not responding as quickly as you would like, here is a sure fire, and seldom used, method to overcome the resistance you are encountering. We could more accurately call this "the pause that tumesces."

❍ Stop for a moment, but don't just drop your penis carelessly. Very lovingly and gently release it.

❍ Next, do something, such as putting a little more lubricant on your hands and sensuously warm it up.

❍ When you are ready, resume by gently picking up your penis and begin again to slowly stroke upward, applying more pressure at the bottom and lightening up as you near the top. Each time you "pause," you will be able to achieve a new level when you resume.

❍ When your penis becomes fully erect, continue to use an up and down rhythmic milking motion, going from the base up to the ridge of the head of your penis, or even slightly over the head. Remember to continue to use slightly heavier pressure at the bottom, and lighten your pressure as you get to the top.

Some men only pay attention to the "up" stroke. However, there is as much sensation available on the "down" stroke as the up. Make sure you are feeling both the up and the down.

The Two-handed Method

❍ Experiment by using both hands. Stroke up and down on your penis, one hand above the other, as if you were holding a baseball bat. Allow your top hand to slip off the top of the penis without losing contact with your bottom hand. Then slide both hands downward to the base of your penis and begin to come back up again.

❍ As you feel your excitement begin to build up, either change the stroke, lighten the pressure you are using, or stop altogether.

❍ Stroke different parts of your penis, including the sides, to discover what feels best to you. Which part of your penis feels the best when you touch or stroke it?

❍ Experiment by altering the kind of strokes you use…faster, slower, firmer, lighter, shorter, longer, etc. When you are stroking your penis, which pressure feels best to you? Light? Heavy? When you are stroking your penis, which speed feels best to you? Slow? Fast?

Do you notice that the more tumesced or excited you become, the more pressure you can pleasantly take?

Peaking

"Peaking" is a technique that is designed to increase your ability to feel more than you presently do.

As you continue the sexercise and your tumescence builds, bring yourself as close to the upper side of that feeling as is possible without going over the top…then let yourself down and regain control by trying one of the following methods: Stopping…Slowing down…Changing to a lighter pressure, or...Changing the direction you are rubbing.

Notice that each time you build up to the edge, the intensity of the feeling increases. If you continue to do this, you will be able to build the intensity to the highest point possible.

On a graph, peaking would look like this:

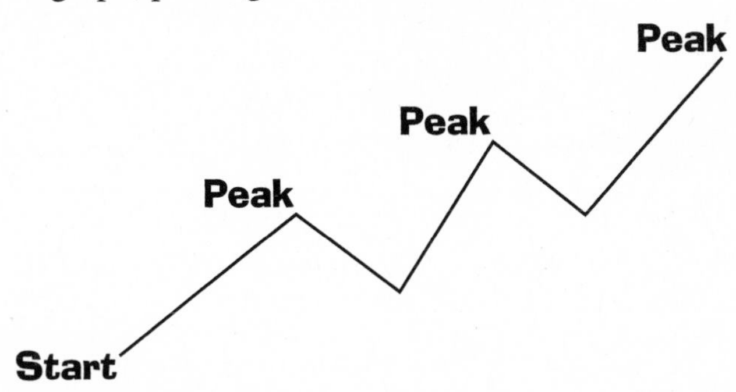

Notice that on the graph, the peaks keep going up to higher levels. Without "Peaking" you could not get to those levels.

Keep "Peaking" yourself as long as it is pleasurable to you. Remember, your goal right now is to feel as good as possible for as long as possible.

Important: Do not go over the top while doing this sexercise. If you become too excited...stop until you regain control.

Right now, you are going for the longest and most pleasurable effect, not ejaculation.

An orgasm causes the release of built-up sexual energy or tumescence. The more you put into the "peaking" of your orgasm, the more sexual energy or tumescence you will release. Your orgasmic contractions will last longer and be stronger than they have ever been before.

Connecting

"Connecting" is sexual stimulation without direct genital contact. It's learning to feel pleasure in the genital area when being kissed or touched in other (secondary) places of your body such as your lips, neck, or ears.

Once you get an area turned on and connected, you can bring yourself or your partner to at least the edge of an orgasm using only the secondary area.

You can "connect" any two areas of your body or your partner's body using the following technique.

❍ Lightly apply warmed Vaseline to another place on your body. Start with your lips.

❍ Continue to rub on your penis and at the same time begin to "tease" your lips by slowly stroking the outside edges using wide circles.

❍ Let your fingers move gradually toward your lips. Once you begin touching them, they should be very excited and turned on.

❍ At the same time, rub your penis with the *same* pressure and movement you are using on your lips. See if you can duplicate the feelings you are having in one area in the other.

❍ Take your hand off your penis and see if it can feel any of the sensations you are creating in your lips.

❍ After a while, begin to rub on your penis again using the same pressure and movement as you are using on your lips.

❍ Now, take your hand off your lips and see if they can feel any of the sensations you are creating in your penis.

Keep switching back and forth until you feel you have gone as far as you can for now.

Do this "connecting" exercise using as many parts of your body as is pleasurable for you.

Try the following areas and write down between 1 (low sensations) to 10 (extremely high sensations) the response you are able to create between the parts you are using: Once you get an area turned on and connected, see if you can bring yourself to the edge of an orgasm using only the secondary area.

❍ The middle toe of your left or right foot ___

❍ Just your upper lip ___

❍ Your ear lobe ___

❍ The inside of your elbow ___

❍ The inside of your thigh ___

❍ The outer part of your penis opening ___

❍ The arch of your foot ___

❍ Your nipples* ___

**Men have the same amount of nerve endings in their nipples as women do. What feels pleasurable to a woman's nipples will most likely feel the same to you. Also, if twisting or pinching real hard when you are not highly aroused feels painful to you, it will probably also feel painful to her.*

Do this sexercise as long as it feels good, continuing to "peak" yourself until the pleasurable feelings you were having are starting to go down or even bottom out.

At any time that you stop having good feelings from stroking yourself…stop! Just say out loud to yourself, ***"This concludes the sexercise."***

If you go too far and cannot stop yourself from having an orgasm during the exercise, before you orgasm say out loud, ***"This concludes the sexercise."***

What is the level of your sexual tension or tumescence? Low? High? Totally flat?

When you are ready, wash the lubricant off your hands, take a few moments to lie still and be aware of how each part of your body is feeling.

Chapter Eight

How Did You Do?

The purpose of Chapter 7 was to impart some crucial information. You learned that, in order to master the "Venus Butterfly" technique, it must be experienced, not merely read.

Please write out the answers to these questions:

1. After doing your "Venus Butterfly" Sexercises, are you now more aware of which parts of your body give you the most pleasure? Write down specifically which parts (lips, neck, nipples, genitals, etc.) and what kind of touching you discovered that you like best:

____

____

____

____

____

2. Now that you are more familiar with your own body, if you were to guess, where might your partner's favorite places be?

____

____

____

____

____

3. Have you learned so far what might help you in pleasuring your partner?

____

____

____

____

____

4. What effects do you suppose practicing your "Venus Butterfly" Sexercises once a week on yourself will have on your relationship with your partner?

____

____

____

____

____

5. What thoughts or considerations stopped you from doing more for yourself during your "Venus Butterfly" Sexercises?

____

____

____

____

____

6. Write down specific dates when you will repeat all of the above "Visiting Dignitary" sexercises for yourself. It is important to repeat these sexercises at least once a week for the next 12 weeks, especially if you are interested in having more control over your sensual nervous system and more intense and longer orgasms.

You will probably resist repeating these exercises, not because you don't want the benefits promised, but because part of us always resists having too much pleasure. The solution is very simple. The first step is to just stop doing the behavior which holds you back.

First, write down the next 12 specific dates and times you will repeat these sexercises over the next three months:

1. ________________
2. ________________
3. ________________
4. ________________
5. ________________
6. ________________
7. ________________
8. ________________
9. ________________
10. ________________
11. ________________
12. ________________

Next, go to your calendar or appointment book and mark the dates when you will repeat these sexercises. Begin to look forward to the next "date" as if it were with the most important person in the world. Because it is!

Sometime in the future you may want your partner to help you do the "Venus Butterfly" sexercises. If you start to slip back into your resisting patterns of behavior, your partner's support may get you back on track. If this kind of support would be valuable, make a date with your partner, and put it on your calendar.

Show And Tell

❍ Make an appointment (date and time) with your partner to talk about how the experience of "Venus Butterfly"sex-ercises were for each of you from beginning to end. (______________________)

❍ Using your notes, go over each detail and be specific with each other on what sensitive areas you discovered.

> **If you can talk openly about one of the most emotionally-charged subjects in the world...sex, you can talk to each other about anything!**

❍ Give each other all the information on how your body works. Eagerly press each other for details. You are gathering information that is necessary in order to have more fun as a couple and to be able to satisfy your partner every time. Pressing yourselves to "talk" to each other about this subject is more important than you can imagine.

❍ Tell each other if you became a little uncomfortable with the amounts of pleasure you were experiencing while you were doing the "Visiting Dignitary" sexercise.

If you became uncomfortable and stopped early, what were the specific thoughts or feelings that caused you to stop? Write your answers below.

____

____

____

____

____

Another purpose of these "Venus Butterfly" sexercises is to begin to increase the amount of pleasure you can physically, emotionally, and mentally enjoy at one stretch.

Has your "pleasure limit" increased by doing the sexercises? If so, in what specific ways?

____

____

____

____

____

Approximately, how many times did you "peak" yourself? ____

Which feelings or thoughts did you experience when you "peaked" yourself?

___ Relaxed?

___Peaceful?

___Anxious?

___More tension?

___Anything else?___________________________

In what specific ways were you able to control, either upward or downward, the sexual energy or tumescence in your body?

____

____

____

____

____

Are some of the "connections" you set up still working? Can you rub some specific, sensitized part of your body and still feel the pleasurable sensations in your genital area? If so, where?

____

____

____

____

____

Great Phone Sex

If you ever find yourself separated from your partner, doing the "Venus Butterfly" sexercises over the phone with each other is great "phone sex." It can make you feel connected even though you may be thousands of miles apart.

Additional Benefits of the "Venus Butterfly" Sexercises

The "Venus Butterfly" sexercises are also very, very beneficial if you are single and want to find or begin to get ready to have a successful relationship. Many people who have begun to practice the "Venus Butterfly" sexercises have reported that the "Handsome Prince" or "Fairy Princess" that they had been looking for seemed to magically show up. We believe this can be best explained by the old saying, "When you are really ready, they will appear."

By practicing the "Venus Butterfly" sexercises on a regular basis, you will begin to allow yourself to experience more fun and spontaneity in your life, both in and out of the bedroom.

Now you are ready to begin using the "Venus Butterfly" technique on your partner.

Chapter Nine

Setting Up The Special "Venus Butterfly" Date

The "Venus Butterfly" date actually begins long before you physically touch each other. To accomplish the intensity, duration, and pleasure of experience that is possible, it is mandatory that total attention be focused on just one of you at a time.

It is more reasonable for the woman to be taken on the "Venus Butterfly" date first. However, since many women will read this book before their partners, there is nothing wrong with the man being taken on the "date" first. The following instructions assume that the man will be taking his partner on the "date."

❍ To start, tell your partner that you are taking her on a special romantic adventure, and announce the date and time. Tell her in such a way as to begin to get her excited. *Make sure you have her undivided attention when you tell her about the* "Venus Butterfly" *date.*

❍ Do this now, and write down exactly when you have scheduled your first date: ____________________

❍ Next, if the date is far enough off, leave her love notes so she will get more and more excited about the date. Put the notes where she will stumble across them, such as on the refrigerator door or on her pillow.

❍ If you have time, mail her a romantic card or note. The note could say something like, "Our date will be one that you will never forget." "I'm going to take you to heights you have never been to before," or, "Remember, our date is only a few hours (days) away." You can even remind her of a special moment you once shared and tell her this time is going to be even better. Include a "Thank You" for something she has done for you and remember to tell her what she means to you.

❍ Send or leave her small presents or flowers with a card attached.

❍ Make an unexpected phone call just to say how much you love her and how much you are looking forward to your date.

"Venus Butterfly" Date Checklist

Prior to the time the date, make sure that all details are taken care of: Use the following checklist to make sure you don't leave anything out. This makes it easier for you to pull everything together. Start on your list now and add to it as you think of more items.

❍ Her favorite romantic music,
❍ Candles,
❍ Something wonderful for her to drink and munch on,
❍ Body lotion or massage oil,
❍ Vaseline,
❍ The room perfectly arranged, and
❍ Your fingernails manicured so that they are rounded with no sharp edges.

Write down anything else you need to do, and the time it needs to be done.

____

____

____

____

As your "Venus Butterfly" date approaches, you will most likely run into a few snags or even some resistance. Not to worry. Just make believe that everything that happens is perfect. You need not force or hurry anything. Just let events unfold at their own pace, even if it means slowing things down or postponing the date so that neither of you feels rushed or pressured. But, once you have promised the "Venus Butterfly" date, go through with it no matter what.

For example, she may be preoccupied with something else and may treat the date with something less than wide-eyed excitement. In that case, it may be a good idea to talk to her about rescheduling the date. Don't do this in a heavy-handed way or else she may blow up at you. Stay light about it. The main thing is for you to stay in charge and totally confident that everything will happen at the right time.

Total Effect

For this ""Venus Butterfly" Date" to work perfectly, you must put her at "total effect," which means that you are "doing" the "Venus Butterfly" technique to her and she is being "done" without expending any energy.

Lovingly stop her if she tries to help at any point during the date. You handle all decisions, phone calls, emergencies, and everything else that comes up in a way that you know will please her.

Do Your Homework

Your homework will involve completing this chapter and reading the sections in Chapter 7 that apply to your partner. Men will read pages 73-76 in the **Sexercises For Men Only** section, and women will read pages 70-73 in the **Sexercises For Women Only** section.

Become very familiar with the body parts of your partner which are described in these sections. Pay special attention to the individual parts of your partner's genitals. Get to know them and their names as well as you do the parts of your own body.

If you are a man, go to the next chapter and proceed to follow the instructions.

If you are a woman, skip the next chapter and go the Chapter 11 entitled **Doing The "Venus Butterfly" To Him**.

Chapter Ten

Doing The "Venus Butterfly" To Her

Creating The Most Intense and Pleasurable Experience Possible

Now that you have everything set up, begin to build and take control of her mood, her five senses, and her tumescence or sexual energy. This will begin right after you make the "Venus Butterfly" date with her and continue right up to the time the "date" ends.

- Bring or send her some flowers and perhaps include taking her on a shopping trip to buy a small gift or sexy lingerie.

- Arrange to fix her a romantic meal or take her to a special restaurant.

Imagine that you are moving all the excitement you have been building in her brain down into her genital area. The easiest way to do this is to directly stimulate the most sensitive nerve endings of her body.

- Having previously made sure that the bedroom is ready, take her there.

- Go very slowly. Start by kissing her slowly and softly in a way that lets her know you are in charge. Start by kissing her forehead, then cheeks, nose, and finally her lips. Do not let her kiss you back unless you want her to. You are the kisser. She is being kissed.

- Begin to slowly remove her clothes. Totally focus on her and talk to her sweetly. Tell her all the things that you love about her skin and her body or, undress her in complete silence and sweetly "forbid" her to say anything. Do what feels good to you and it will almost always be pleasurable to your mate.

- When you are finished undressing her, give her a sensual bath or shower. Make sure this was on your checklist and is set up and ready.

You can be undressed also or you could even be wearing a tuxedo or a pirate suit. Do whatever is going to be fun for you.

- After the bath or shower dry her off with towels scented with a fragrance or perfume she likes and perhaps even pre-warmed in the clothes dryer.

- Next, take her to the bed and ask her to lie down on her back.

- Whatever she is lying on is going to get oil on it, so you may want to put towels under the sheet or have her lie directly on the towels.

- Make sure she is comfortable and warm. You can cover her with a sheet or warm dry towels.

- Take off any rings or jewelry you may be wearing.

- Put some massage oil or body lotion in your hands and warm it up by rubbing your hands together before applying it to her body.

- Start with her feet. Remember to take "taking touches" as you did when you were doing yourself during "tactile inventory." If it feels good to your hand, it will probably feel good to her.

The feet are very sensitive and have a lot of nerve endings that can give great pleasure. Women have reported having orgasms just from having their feet rubbed. Tell her this and let her know that she can enjoy anything that you do to her as much as she wants.

- Stroke the arch of her foot back and forth from the ball of her foot to the heel. Also, try the middle toe of each foot. Any woman can learn to feel stimulation in her clitoris when her feet are rubbed. Ask her to see how much she can feel of what you are doing to her foot or toes in her clitoris.

Apply enough pressure to give her pleasure without tickling her, or causing pain. All through the massage try to find just the right touch by talking to her and having her tell you what feels best to her.

All the way through this process, allow yourself to feel the good feelings that she is experiencing. Imagine that you are able to feel what she is feeling at the same time in your own body. Practicing this technique is going to be very important when you get to her genital area.

In the beginning of the courses at More University, the professors sometimes call the men "Hammer Hands." They do this because most men have never been taught how to feel what their partner is feeling. Learning to feel what she is feeling is one of the most important ways to increase your sexual and sensual skills.

By practicing the method in this book you will develop a "velvet touch." You will learn to feel when her sensations are rising and when they begin to taper off. You will feel the contractions of her orgasm and learn how to intensify and extend her orgasmic contractions for as long as it is fun for both of you.

When you master this technique you will enjoy the sensations she is having almost as much as she does, and feel her sensations in your own body.

- As you are touching her and moving from one area to another, make sure you are staying in communication with her. Do this from the very beginning of the "Venus Butterfly" date.

- Tell her what you are going to do before you do it. If you need to stop to put some more oil on your hands, remember to let her know ***before*** you stop massaging. When you are warming the oil up in your hands, say, "I'm warming the oil up in my hands before I put it on you. Now it's warm enough and I'm going to spread it on your skin."

- Get feedback from her as to exactly what feels the best to her.

- Inform her of what you are doing, step by step, so she doesn't have to think or try to figure it out. There is no need to tell her anything except what the next step is.

- Next, take her hand and begin to work on her fingers, working up her hands, then arms, and on to the front of her shoulders and her chest.

- Begin to make circles around the outermost curve of her breasts. Be careful not to touch the nipples. They may be too sensitive and cause her discomfort if you touch them directly or before they are ready.

- Slowly begin to make the circles smaller and smaller as if you are teasing the nipples. Make them want to be touched.

- When you think they are ready and she is expecting them to be touched, tell her that you are now going to go back to caressing the outside rim of her breasts and slowly do so.

- Keep teasing her breasts until you feel her level of tumescence build up to a very high level and touching her nipples comes naturally.

Some women have very sensitive nipples and you should use a lot of lubricant. You may even need to put a piece of thin cloth over her and touch her nipples through the cloth. Just make sure that you touch them in a way that gives her the most pleasure.

- When her nipples have had enough, begin to work on the fronts of her thighs and her stomach.

Only when you have shown all her other parts of her body enough attention should you begin to tease her genital area.

- Start making circles slowly around her pubic area with the tips of your fingers without touching her pubic hairs.

- Make your circles smaller and smaller until you are

barely touching the outer edge of her hairline. Her hairs are an extension of her skin. Run your hand over the tops of her pubic hairs, touching them lightly, and ask her if she likes the sensations.

As she becomes excited, you may notice that her pubic hairs stand up, reaching upward as if they want to be touched. Also, when she becomes turned on, the lips around her vagina will open up by themselves.

The Official "Venus Butterfly" Positions

At this point you need to decide what position would be most comfortable as you proceed. It is important that you be comfortable during this entire process. If you are not, your partner will pick up your stress, which will decrease the amount of pleasure you both experience.

- First make sure she is lying comfortably on her back with her legs spread apart.

The best position to use, if you are right-handed, is to sit beside her on her left side with your right leg, your leg nearest her head, over her stomach. Your left leg, the leg nearest her feet, will go under her legs.

Doing The "Venus Butterfly" To Her

Reverse this if you are left-handed. You will be on her right side and your left leg would go over her stomach. Your right leg will go under her legs.

Using this "Venus Butterfly" position, you can easily use both hands, and at the same time see what you are doing. Most men can comfortably stay in this position for long periods of time. To make sure you stay comfortable, it is a good idea to prop large pillows behind and beside you. Support your back by leaning against the pillows, headboard, or a wall next to the bed.

Other Positions

1. Sit beside her with your leg, the one nearest her head, bent so that you are sitting on your foot, or so that your bent leg is slightly in front of you and pressing against the side of her body. Your other leg, the one nearest her feet, will be under her legs or crossed in front of you. If you are right-handed, you will still be on her left side. If you are left-handed, you will be on her right side. In this position it is also a good idea to prop large pillows beside and behind you. Support your back by leaning against the pillows, headboard, or a wall next to the bed.

2. Kneel beside her. Approach her from her left side if you are right-handed. If you are left-handed, you will be on her right side. This position may become tiresome after a while and begin to hurt your knees, but it allows you to keep eye contact and talk to her easily.

3. Lie beside her with your head toward her feet. Your bottom arm over her leg, holding yourself up by putting your weight on your elbow. Be on her left side if you are right-handed. If you are left-handed be on her right side. Using this position, you can easily use both hands as well as see what you are doing. You will be stimulating her clitoris using the hand of your free arm.

- When you are ready, tell her to spread her legs so that you can apply Vaseline* to her genital area.

*Vaseline is not water soluble, so not even perspiration will wash it off. It also spreads and *radiates* pleasurable sensations. Vaseline seems to have a preferable consistency and creates a unique "drag" effect even though it is made of basically the same ingredients as other brands. After your first "Venus Butterfly" date, you can try other brands, to see which one you prefer.

(Note: Do not use Vaseline or any petroleum based product if you are concerned about the spread of a sexually transmitted disease. If you are not totally sure that both you and your partner are totally free of sexually transmittable diseases, use a water based product and latex gloves while using this technique. See Chapter 13 for more information.)

- After warming the lubricant up with your hands, begin to slowly and gently spread it on:

1. the outer lips of her vagina (labia majora),

2. then her inner lips (labia minora),

3. then the opening to her vagina. Not up inside her vagina, just on the opening.

4. Finally, follow the inner lips up to the point that they begin to form the hood over her clitoris. Carefully and slowly lubricate the hood of her clitoris and very gently include the head of the clitoris (clitoral glans) itself.

A woman's clitoris is very similar to the shaft of a man's penis and its end, the clitoral glans, is like the crown or end of a man's penis. The hood of the clitoris is like his foreskin.

You can think of the penis as a large clitoris and the clitoris as a small penis.

Diagram of The Female Genital Area

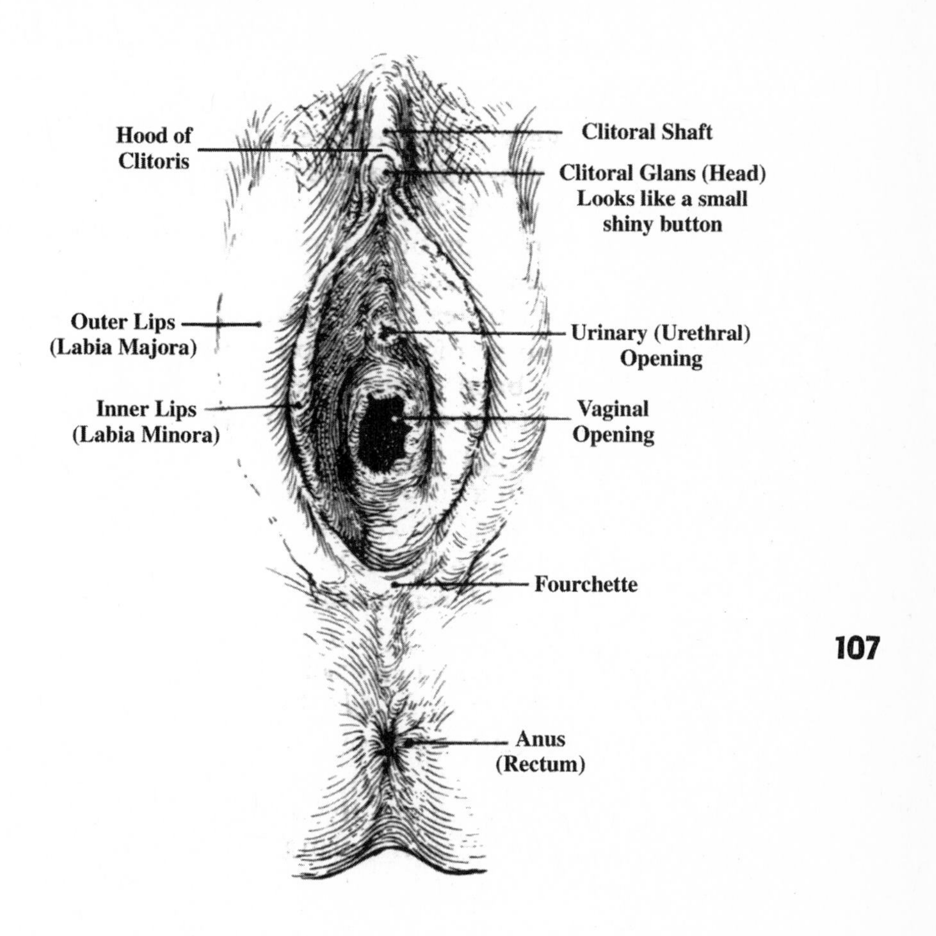

As you are applying lubricant, ask her to spread her fingers and toes to feel sensations throughout her whole body. Most women report that when they do this, they experience more intense sensations.

- Use a lot of Vaseline. Vaseline spreads sensation and prevents skin irritation from long periods of love making. It also allows you to easily use both heavy or light pressure.

• Talking to her as you go along can help to turn her on. Tell her how beautiful, radiant, and exciting she is, and let her know you could touch her this way all night long.

Almost all women love to hear over and over how much they turn you on and how beautiful they are to the man they love. They never get tired of hearing real compliments about their attractiveness, any more than you get tired of being told by her how well you did when you accomplished something.

Master The Possibilities

There are two possibilities a man can use while he is doing the two-handed "Venus Butterfly" to a woman.

The Two-hand Position

When you use the two-hand position, have her raise her hips, keeping her legs open so that, using your hand which is nearest her feet with your fingers spread wide apart, you can reach underneath her buttocks.

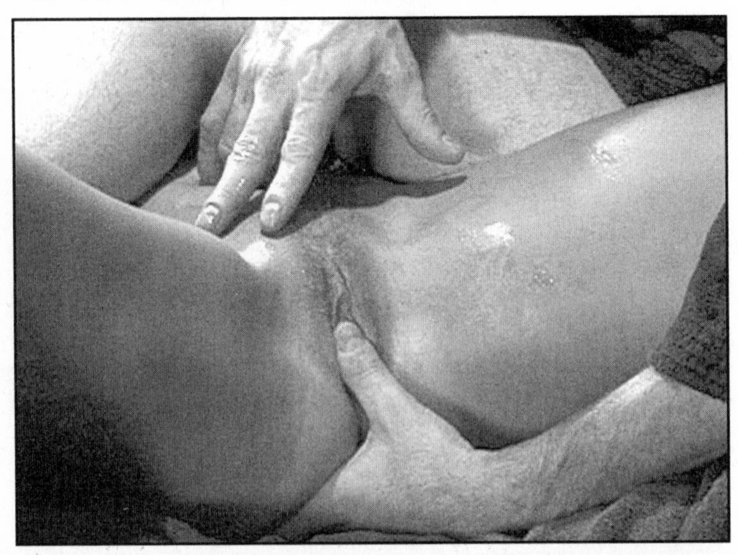

Spread your middle and ring fingers wide apart so that her spine can rest comfortably between those two fingers while the thumb of your bottom hand presses against her vaginal opening. Do not insert your thumb inside of her. Let your thumb rest lightly and snugly over the opening.

Make sure that your bottom hand feels comfortable to both of you and that you are *gently* holding her firmly and securely.

The Advanced Two-hand Position

The thumb of your bottom hand will rest lightly and snugly on her vaginal opening as in the two-hand position, but at the same time your middle finger is resting lightly on her anus. Do not insert your finger inside of her. Just let your finger rest firmly and snugly against her anus.

The "Honeysuckle"

In the either of the above positions, as she begins to have pleasurable sensations, you may feel one or both of your fingers being sucked in to one or both of her openings. We call this phenomenon the "Honeysuckle." Until this happens on its own, do not attempt to press your fingers inside of her. Just let them rest gently on the outside.

Some men use a latex examination glove on one or both hands. Do whatever is the most appropriate for you. The use of latex gloves is discussed more fully in Chapter 13.

Make It Want To Be Touched

- Now that you are in a comfortable position, begin to use your free hand to "take" pleasuring strokes. Don't start at the focal point, the clitoris, but instead begin at the outermost part of an imaginary circle around the clitoris and begin to work your way toward it.

You are attempting to excite her clitoris. Make it want to be touched. Tease it as long as possible before you finally give it any direct pleasure.

- Start by slowly and gently stroking her outer lips,

- Then her inner lips,

- Get every bit of pleasure you can from each part before going on to the next.

- Next, around the opening of her vagina above your thumb,

- And finally directly up from the vagina opening to the middle ridge, which is her clitoris.

Her Love Button

An easy way to find the most sensitive part of a woman's genitals, her clitoris, is to start at the vaginal opening and go straight up until you feel a bump. That's it.

- When you get to her clitoris, lightly pull one side of the hood back using the side of your thumb. Then to keep her clitoris from moving around, "anchor" it in place by gently pressing the side of your thumb down along the side of her clitoris.

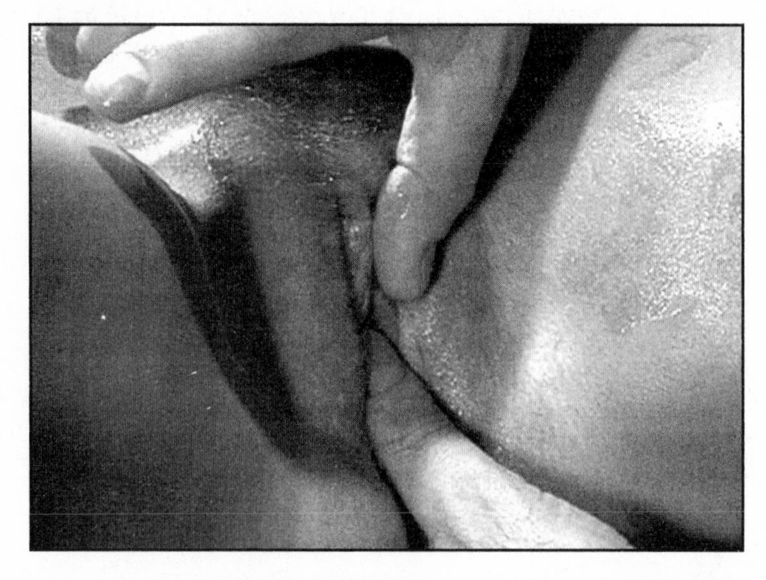

- The rest of your fingers will be pointing down toward her vaginal opening. Reach down with your middle finger and begin to find the area on or around the clitoris which gives her the most pleasure.

- Start very slowly with a very light up and down movement, the "bread and butter" stroke. Imagine that your finger is a delicate butterfly wing that is slowly, lovingly, and sensuously stroking up and down over her most delicate nerve endings.

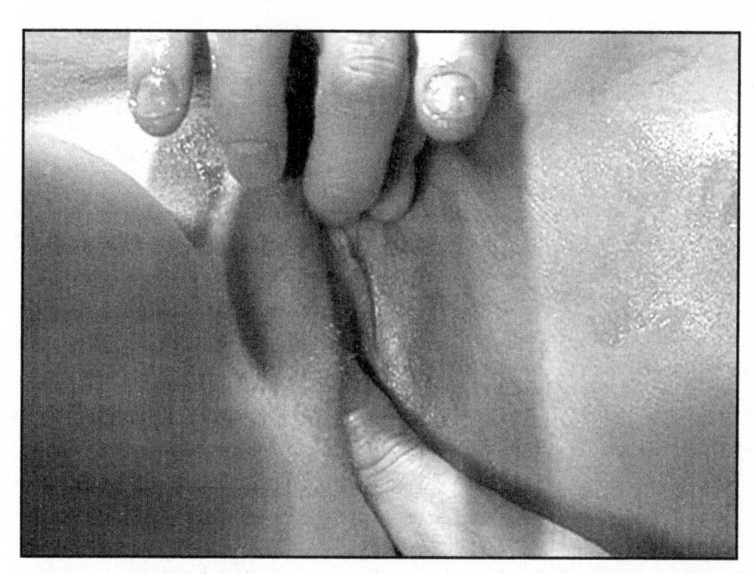

- From time to time you can stop for a moment and take a look at her clitoris to make sure you are on the right spot. Sometimes you will find that you have slipped off the clitoris and are rubbing on her hood or somewhere else. Visual confirmation will give you certainty and build your confidence.

Most men sometimes only pay attention to the "up" "Venus Butterfly" stroke. However, there is as much sensation available on the "down" stroke as the up. Check with her to make sure she is feeling both the up and the down strokes.

Sometimes, until she is very excited, the head of the clitoris may be too sensitive to stimulate directly even with very, very light pressure. If this is the case, add more lubricant or begin to build her excitement by touching only the hood which surrounds her clitoris. If even lighter pressure is required, touch only the lubricant and let the ripples of sensation spread into her most sensitive areas.

As you feel her tumescence build to a critical point, remind her to spread her fingers and toes to feel sensations throughout her body.

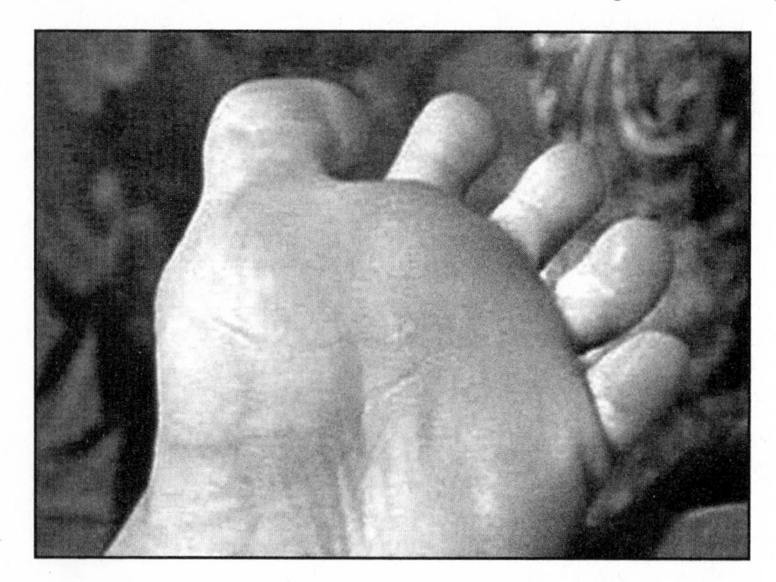

- Don't let her go over the top yet. To bring her down and regain control, either change the stroke you are using from up and down to side to side…or lighten the pressure you are using…or stop all together for just one or two strokes. Always tell her what you are doing before you do it.

Discover the Most Sensitive Part of her Clitoris

Most women will have slightly more feeling on one side of their clitoris than on the other. When you start out, she will probably think that her right side is more sensitive. The main reason for this is that most women are right handed and usually stimulate themselves with their right hand. This may cause her to favor the right side of the clitoris, but there is a place on her left side that has more potential if developed.

For many women it is best to start at the 10 o'clock position (looking head on at her genitals) and slowly work toward their most sensitive spot which is at about 1 o'clock.

The "Communications Cycle"

Your goal during this process is to give your partner the most intense pleasurable feelings possible. The easiest way to accomplish this every time is to use what we call the More University "Communication" or "Training Cycle." With this technique you can find out exactly where, when, and how to give your partner precisely what she wants, when she wants it, for as long as she wants.

When you are doing the "Venus Butterfly" to your partner, you need to know, at all times, if you are making contact with the correct spot, with the right amount of pressure. The only way you can know this for sure is to ask, but you must be careful not to make your partner lose touch with what she is feeling.

By communicating, you will learn the perfect amount of pressure and speed to use with each series of strokes without having your partner lose the mood.

The secret is to ask simple, short, yes or no questions which can be answered without too much thought. For example:

1. "Would you like me to rub harder than this?" (Answer, "Yes.")

2. "Okay," you say as you increase the pressure. "Would you like it harder than this?" (Answer, again "Yes.")

3. "Okay," you say as you increase the pressure even more. "Would you like it harder than this?" (Answer, "No.")

4. "Okay. Would you like it softer than this?" (If you get a "No" at this point, you are right on the mark. Just continue to use that pressure. If you get a "*Yes*," keep decreasing the pressure until your partner lets you know you are doing great.

This technique is very effective in finding the right spot on the clitoris or on any part of her body and discovering which exact amount of pressure or speed feels best. "To the left more?" … "Higher?" … "Would you like a faster stroke?" … "Slower?" … "More lubricant?" …etc.

On some women, the clitoris is hard to find and stay in contact with. It might keep slipping away from you. Don't worry or let her get upset. You are just one step away from finding it with the "Training Cycle."

If you get off the right spot for even one stroke, let her know that you want her to say so immediately. Here is what you should ask her to do so that you are always pleasing her.

Ask her if she would she be willing to follow just three simple steps.

1. At anytime that she wants you to do something different, the first step is for her to acknowledge your overall actions. She simply says, "That's great!" or "This feels so wonderful!"

2. Next, she makes a request of you that will bring her even more pleasure. It is a small step that you can easily fulfill. She could say, "Will you…(one of the following)

…go slower?" (faster?)

…rub a little softer?" (harder?)

…come up a little higher?" (down a little lower?)

…move your finger a little to the left?" (right?)

…stop for a moment?"

…give me a drink of water?"

…move your finger up and down?"

…move your finger from side to side?"

…use more lubricant?"

By making a simple request, she is furnishing you with the information that you need so that you can give her exactly what will please her the most. This way you don't have to guess or shoot in the dark.

3. As soon as you respond to her request, then she says, "That's even better!" or "That's wonderful! Thank you."

Now you know that you are improving and that she appreciates your commitment to pleasing her. Each time, she makes a request, she follows all three steps. This is her version of the Training Cycle when she is the one receiving pleasure.

Sex is one of the most difficult subjects couples attempt to communicate about. These training cycles will help her communicate more easily and effectively about what she really wants.

A good "test" to see if she is paying attention to how much she is feeling is to tell her you are going to stop for just a moment.

- Immediately resume and do 10 strokes on her.

- Stop again and ask her how many strokes did she feel since you stopped a few moments ago. If she says 5, then she is only feeling 50% of the sensation that it is possible for her to feel.

Throw this "test" in every once in a while to check on her improvement.

The One Hour Orgasm

When you are doing the "Venus Butterfly" to her the first time, she may beg you to let her go over the top. Do not do this until you are ready for her to go. Tell her over and over that everything will be all right, just relax and maybe next time you will let her go. Slow her down. Don't rush. You have all night if you want.

- Hold out as long as possible. You can switch to rubbing on her outer or inner lips. It will be pleasurable, but she will probably want you back on the clitoris as quickly as possible.

- Don't let her rush you. You are in charge and will get her there in due time.

Include time to "connect up" other parts of her body with her clitoris. Basically, you are to rub on some other part of her body, such as her breasts, which contain a large number of nerve endings and create a sympathetic response in her clitoris.

- Tell her you are going to begin to rub on the nipple of her breast at the same time you are stroking her clitoris.

- Once she is feeling pleasurable sensations in both areas, tell her that you are going to stop rubbing on her clitoris, but you want her to see if she can "feel" the touching you are doing to her nipple in her clitoris.

- After a while, inform her that you are once again going to stroke her clitoris. Stop rubbing on her nipple and ask her to see if she can "feel" the touching you are doing to her clitoris in her nipple.

- Keep going back and forth until you have set up a connection between the two. Stop whenever either of you get tired of doing this.

The most common areas that seem to lend themselves favorably to being connected are the areas used in petting such as her lips, neck, stomach, the inside of her legs, her knees, as well as her breasts and nipples.

Other areas with large bundles of nerve endings, such as the middle toe, the anus, and just inside the vagina opening can also be explored.

Size Doesn't Matter

If done properly, just one inch of penetration inside her vagina can be felt by her as far up as 12 inches or more. Here's what you need to do:

- As you are stroking her clitoris, gently feel around the opening to her vaginal canal. Don't go very far up inside of her just yet. Ask her to tell you how far she can feel your finger inside of her.

- Next, insert your finger inside her vaginal canal and press or stroke her vaginal wall at the 3, 6, 9, and 12 o'clock positions. As you're doing this, ask her which spots, and what pressure and speed feels best to her.

The "G-Spot"

The 12 o'clock position is interesting because it is directly behind her clitoris and enables you to make her feel as if you are stimulating her clitoris from another side. This area, which is about the size of a button and gets hard as the woman gets excited, is sometimes referred to as the G-Spot.

Most men are confused by the G-Spot because they act as if they think that it works like a garage door opener.

Their bewilderment is caused by the ignorance of the little known fact that rubbing or pressing on this spot does not work except after she is already highly aroused or close to climaxing. After she is sufficiently aroused, this spot acts like a turbo charger and can greatly increase the intensity of her orgasmic sensations.

Take Her Over The Top

At some point you will be ready to take her over the top. You will have been keeping her in an orgasmic state as close to the edge as you have wanted to.

- Remember to tell her what you are going to do before you do it. You might even use this opportunity to peak her some more.

- You can even play with her in a way that increases her tumescence. Tell her that, just for fun, she has only twenty seconds to go over the top, and if she doesn't make it you are going to bring her down one more time.

She will probably choke up under the pressure and not make it. That's fine. Every time you peak her, you build up the pressure of the climax and take it to a level that would not have been possible without peaking.

One Hour Orgasms

All during your "Venus Butterfly" date you should strive to get her to have orgasmic contractions and sensations without going over the top. This is also the key to a woman's ability to have orgasmic contractions that last up to an hour.

Just remember, her orgasm comes from intense, pleasurable, contractions. With practice, you can cause her to have hundreds, even thousands of orgasmic contractions, of varying intensity, during a "Venus Butterfly" lovemaking session.

- As you continue, and her tumescence builds, bring her as close to the edge as is possible without going over the top. Then bring her down and regain control by trying one of the following methods: Stopping; Slowing way down; Changing to a much lighter pressure; Changing the direction you are rubbing, or; Changing the rhythm you are using.

- Notice that each time you bring her close to the edge, the intensity of her contractions will increase. Continue to take her to the edge each time, and you will be able to keep her contractions going longer and stronger.

- Each time you feel her tumescence build up to a critical point, remind her to spread her fingers and toes to feel sensations all the way out to those areas. This allows her to spread the sensation throughout her whole body.

With enough practice, you will be able to get her to the top level of orgasm, which we call the "orgasmic state." At this level, she will be having full body contractions, one after the other, and you will be able to keep them going for as long as both of you want.

To reach this orgasmic state, you will need to become proficient using the "Venus Butterfly" technique with total confidence and her nervous system will need to be strengthened so as to be able to reach high levels of intensity without discomfort. Anyone can attain these abilities with enough practice. Just remember the saying, "The way to get to Carnegie Hall is practice, practice, practice."

- At some point she will either slip over the top, or you will deliberately take her there. Once she starts into this final climax phase, stay very alert to what you are feeling, both in your body and in your finger. It is usually time for you to begin to lighten the pressure or else her climax could turn from pleasure to pain. Give her just enough pressure, but not too much. Maintain a steady rhythm and pressure.

You will learn as you practice how much pressure feels the best to her, and when to begin to lighten or increase your stroke.

Notice that her body will pull away from you when you are pressing too hard, and push toward you when she wants more pressure.

- Now the best part. Once she has climaxed totally and has nothing left, there are still pleasurable feelings left over for the taking. All you need to do is to continue to stroke her, using more Vaseline to prevent friction and usually a lighter and slower touch as you bring her down.

Even at this point, she is probably not all of the way detumesced. This means, using our scale of tumescent energy, she would be at a level two or three…not at a level one yet.

- Bring her all of the way down. Do not leave her feeling like she is floating three feet over the bed. You will know you are finished when she is totally "flat." This means there are no more pleasurable sensations left in her.

A good way to end with her is to lie on top of her or even to have intercourse with her. Heavy pressure on her body or chest, will help bring her completely down.

At this point, if you have been allowing yourself to feel what she has been feeling, you may feel as if you have gone through the orgasmic state and climax yourself, and you may feel totally *detumesced.*

- Don't let up at this point. You are still in the process of making love to each other. Being intimate and talking is just as much a part of lovemaking as is touching each other. Have her tell you everything about how the whole "Venus Butterfly" date was for her, from beginning to end. Get her to talk about even the smallest details and be specific as to what pleasurably sensitive areas you discovered on her.

You will be amazed at how much you discover about each other and how exciting being with each other will become. Don't be surprised if you learn something new about each other each time you practice the "Venus Butterfly" technique…no matter how many years you have been together.

How'd You Do?

Well? Did you keep time? Did you keep her orgasmic contractions and sensations going for one hour this session?

Don't worry. In the long run, it doesn't make much difference. How long you can get her to sustain an orgasmic state, or how many contractions you can get her to have, is really not that important.

The most important goal is to see how much pleasure and fun both of you can get out of practicing the "Venus Butterfly" technique.

Training For Your Marathon Of Pleasure

Although it is easy to be patient when you are having fun, think of practicing the "Venus Butterfly" technique and training for your one hour orgasm as if you were training for a marathon.

If you were going to run a marathon, you would not jump up the first day and run 26 miles as hard as you could. You would start out with a mile or two at a slow pace. Later you would increase your distance until you got up to your goal. The same is true in mastering the "Venus Butterfly" technique.

Just keep practicing. Each time you do, you will find yourself going for more fun and pleasure.

You've Got It

The information you have received so far, with practice, will enable you to produce dramatically extended periods of orgasmic contractions in your partner.

However, having an orgasm last an hour or more (no matter how exciting and thrilling the prospect) is not the primary purpose of the "Venus Butterfly" technique. It is a wonderful side benefit.

Our main goal is to teach couples how to have more fun in their relationships and their sex life.

In our videos/DVDs, ***For His Eyes Only*** and ***For Her Eyes Only***, you can see a live demonstrations of the "Venus Butterfly" technique being taught and successfully performed.

Good luck and have lots of fun every chance you get.

Men: Skip past Chapter 11 to Chapter 12 on page 147

Chapter Eleven

Doing The "Venus Butterfly" To Him

Creating The Most Intense and Pleasurable Experience Possible

Now that you have everything set up, begin to build and take control of his mood, his five senses, and his sexual energy. This will begin right after you make the "Venus Butterfly" date with him and will continue right up to the time the "date" ends.

- Start out by bringing or sending him some flowers (men like flowers, too) and even taking him on a shopping trip to buy him a small gift for your "Venus Butterfly" Date.

- Arrange to fix him a romantic meal with his favorite foods or take him to a special restaurant as a prelude to the "Venus Butterfly" date.

Imagine that you are moving all the excitement you have been building in his brain down into his genital area. The easiest way to do this is to directly stimulate the most sensitive nerve endings of his body.

- Having previously made sure the bedroom is ready, take him there.

- Go very slowly. Start by kissing him softly in a way that lets him know you are in charge. Start by kissing his forehead, then cheeks, nose, and finally his lips. Do not let him kiss you back unless you want him to. You are the kisser. He is being kissed.

- Begin to enjoy slowly removing his clothes. Totally focus on him and talk to him sweetly. Tell him all the things that you love about him and his body or, undress him in complete silence and sweetly "forbid" him to say anything. Do what feels good to you and it will almost always be pleasurable to him.

- When you are finished undressing him, give him a sensual bath or shower. Make sure this was on your checklist and is set up and ready.

You can be undressed also or you could wear something that is comfortable and makes you feel sensual and sexy. Undressing slowly to music in front of him might increase the suspense and tumescence you are attempting to build. Do whatever is going to be fun for you.

- After the bath or shower, dry him off with towels scented with a fragrance he likes and perhaps even prewarmed in the clothes dryer.

- Next, take him to the bed and ask him to lie down on his back.

- Whatever he is lying on is going to get oil on it, so you may want to put towels under the sheet or have him lie directly on the towels.

- Make sure he is comfortable and warm. You can cover him with a sheet or warm dry towels.

- Take off any rings or jewelry you may be wearing.

- Put some body lotion or massage oil in your hands and warm it up by rubbing your hands together before applying it to his body.

- Start with his feet. Remember to take "taking touches" as you did when you were doing yourself during "tactile inventory." If it feels good to your hand, it will probably feel good to him.

The feet are very sensitive and have a lot of nerve endings that can give great pleasure.

- Stroke the arch of his foot back and forth from the ball of his foot to the heel. Also, try the middle toe of each foot. A man can learn to feel stimulation in his penis when his feet are rubbed. Ask him to see how much he can feel of what you are doing to his foot or toes in his penis.

- Apply enough pressure to give him pleasure without tickling him, but not enough to cause pain. All through the massage try to find just the right touch by talking to him and having him tell you what feels best to him.

All the way through this process allow yourself to feel the good feelings that he is experiencing. Imagine that you are able to feel what he is feeling at the same time in your own body. Practicing this technique is going to be very important when you get to his genital area.

Learning to feel what he is feeling is one of the most important ways to increase your sexual and sensual skills.

By practicing this method you too will learn to develop a "velvet touch." You will learn to feel when his sensations are rising and when they begin to taper off. You will feel the contractions of his orgasm and learn how to intensify and extend his orgasmic contractions for as long as it is fun for both of you.

When you master this technique you will enjoy the sensations he is having almost as much as he does, and feel his sensations in your own body.

- As you are touching him and moving from one area to another, make sure you are staying in communication with him. Do this from the very beginning of the "Venus Butterfly" date.

- Tell him what you are going to do before you do it. If you need to stop to put some more oil or Vaseline on your hands, remember to let him know *before* you stop. When you are warming the oil up in your hands, say, "I'm warming the oil up in my hands before I put it on you...Now it's warm enough and I'm going to spread it on your skin."

- Get feedback from him as you go along as to exactly what feels the best to him.

- Inform him of what you are doing, step by step, so he doesn't have to think or try to figure it out. There is no need to tell him anything except what the next step is.

- Next, take his hand and begin to work on his fingers, working up his hands, then arms, and on to the front of his shoulders and his chest.

- Begin to make circles around the outermost edges of his chest. Be careful not to touch his nipples. They may be too sensitive and cause him discomfort if you touch them directly or before they are ready.

- Slowly begin to make the circles smaller and smaller as if you are teasing the nipples. Make them want to be touched.

- When you think he is expecting them to be touched, tell him that you are now going to go back to caressing the outside rim of his chest and do so.

- Keep repeating this process of teasing until you can feel the energy of his tumescence and touching his nipples comes naturally.

Some men, like women, have very sensitive nipples and you should use a lot of lubricant. You may even need to put a piece of thin cloth over him and touch his nipples through the cloth. Just make sure that you touch him in a way that gives him the most pleasure.

- When this area has had enough, begin to work on the fronts of his thighs and his stomach.

- Continue to touch that area until you are tired of touching it and then tell him you are moving on to another area.

- Only when you have shown all the above areas enough attention should you begin to tease his genital area. Use light strokes from your fingernails on his lower stomach and the tops of his thighs.

- Next, start making circles slowly around the outside of his pubic hair and penis area with the tips of your fingers. As his excitement increases, you may notice that the hairs around his penis begin to stand up, reaching upward as if they want to be touched.

- The hairs are an extension of the skin. Run your hand over the tops of his pubic hairs, touching them lightly, and ask him if he likes the sensations.

- When you are ready, tell him to spread his legs so that you can apply Vaseline* to his genital area. Use a lot of Vaseline. Vaseline prevents skin irritation from long periods of love making and allows you to easily use both heavy or light pressure.

*Vaseline is not water soluble, so not even perspiration will wash it off. It also spreads and radiates pleasurable sensations. Vaseline seems to have a consistency that is preferable to other brands of petroleum jelly even though it is made of basically the same ingredients. After your first "Venus Butterfly" date you can try other brands, if you like, to see which one you prefer.

(Note: Do not use Vaseline or any petroleum-based product if you are concerned about the spread of a sexually transmitted disease. If you are not totally sure that both you and your partner are totally free of sexually transmittable diseases, use a water based product and latex gloves while using this technique. See Chapter 13 for more information.)

- First, warm the lubricant up with your hands.

- Start on the area away from his penis...his scrotum (the sack that covers his testicles). Be very careful not push upwards on his testicles because this can be very painful.

- Next, continue to gently apply Vaseline until you have covered his penis, his scrotum, his external anal area, and the area between his scrotum and his anus which is called his perineum (pear-i-nee-um). Use plenty of lubricant. Too much is better than too little.

- As you are applying lubricant, ask him to spread his fingers and toes, and feel what you are doing all throughout his body. Most people report that when they do this, it allows them to experience more intense sensations.

- Remember to keep talking to him. Tell him what you are doing and keep asking for feedback. Talking to him as you go along can help to turn him on and make it easier for him to surrender to you.

The Official "Venus Butterfly" Positions

At this point you need to decide what position would be most comfortable for you. It is important that you are comfortable during this entire process. If you are not, your partner will pick up your stress, which will decrease the amount of pleasure you both are having.

There are many positions a woman can use while she is doing the "Venus Butterfly" technique to a man. We will talk about a few of the possibilities, and you can select the one which works best for you.

Make sure he is lying comfortably on his back with his legs spread apart.

> The best position to use, if you are right-handed, is to sit beside him on his left side with your right leg, your leg nearest his head, over his stomach. Your left leg, the leg nearest his feet, will go under his legs.

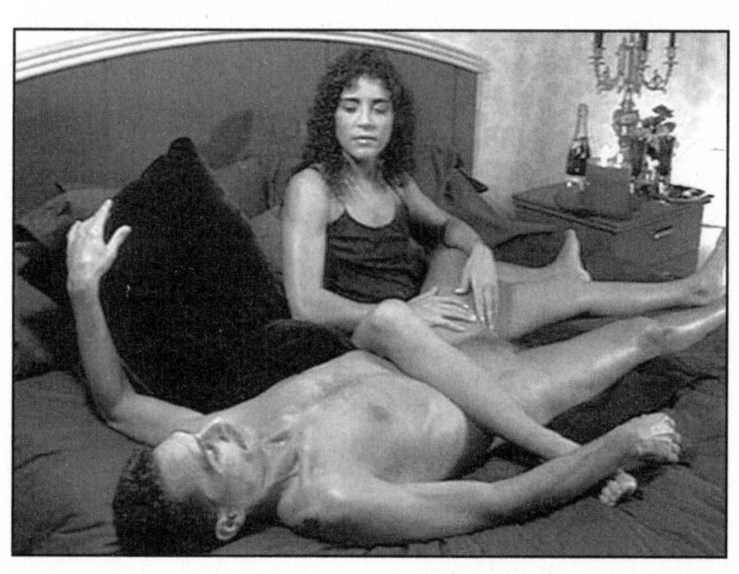

> Reverse the position if you are left-handed. You will be on his right side and your left leg would go over his stomach. Your right leg will go under his legs.

Using this "Venus Butterfly" position, you can easily use both hands and at the same time see what you are doing. Most women can comfortably stay in this position for long periods of time. To make sure you stay comfortable, it is a good idea to prop large pillows behind and beside you. Support your back by leaning against the pillows, headboard, or a wall next to the bed.

Other Positions

1. Kneel or sit between his legs, facing his genitals. Your legs can be crossed, either under or inside his legs. In this position you can see his facial expressions and easily reach his genital area.

2. Lie between his legs with your head on his thigh and his other leg over your body.

3. Lie with his arm around you and with your head resting on his chest. Your top arm reaches straight down to his genitals.

Make It Want To Be Touched

Your partner won't necessarily have an erection when you start even after you have applied lubrication, so start out with the following approach.

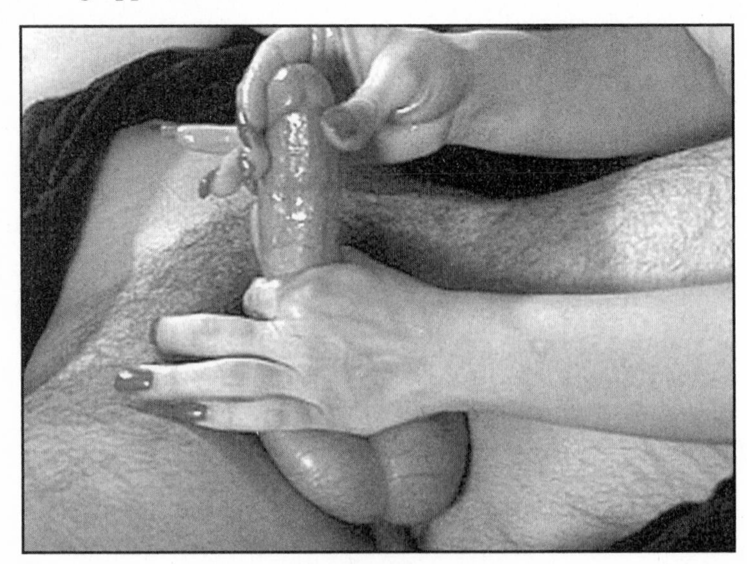

Doing The "Venus Butterfly" To Him

- Make a circle with the thumb and index finger of each of your hands.

- Encircle the shaft of his penis at its base with one hand.

- With your other hand, circle his penis with your thumb and index finger just above your bottom hand.

- Holding your bottom hand firmly at the base of his penis, gently and slowly slide your other hand (top hand) up the shaft. Use a milking motion with your top hand, stretching his penis gently until you reach the top. Apply more pressure at the bottom and lighten up as you near the top. This gentle motion not only feels good to him, it also draws blood into his penis, making it harder and more erect.

- Once your top hand slowly slides over the top of his penis, again form a ring around his penis just above your bottom hand. Once again, move your top hand slowly upward, using your milking motion as you slightly stretch his penis again.

- It may feel good to him if you add a slight twisting movement as your fingers travel up his shaft. Try it at some point and ask him if he likes that motion. Only ask questions that he can answer with a simple yes or no.

- As his penis enlarges, you can use more than two fingers to form your "rings."

• Continue to do this until his penis becomes erect. You will find the above method valuable in persuading his penis to respond any time you want it to, or if you want to harden an already full erection.

The Pause That Refreshes

If he (or his penis) is not responding as quickly as you would like, here is a sure fire and seldom used method to overcome the resistance you are encountering. We could more accurately call this "the pause that tumesces."

- Tell him that you are going to stop for a moment, but don't just drop his penis carelessly. Treat it with respect. Release it very lovingly and gently.

A man thinks of his penis as if it were a small and vulnerable version of him. If you are being sweet and considerate to his penis, you're being sweet and considerate to him.

- Next, do something, such as putting a little more lubricant on your hands and sensuously warm it up by rubbing your hands together slowly, rearranging your pillows, taking or offering him a sip of water.

- When you are ready, resume by gently picking up his penis and begin again to slowly stroke upward, using your milking motion, applying more pressure at the bottom and lightening up as you near the top. Each time you "pause," you will take him to a new level when you resume.

- When his penis becomes fully erect, continue to use your standard up and down rhythmic milking motion on the shaft of his penis, going from the base up to the ridge of the head of his penis, or even slightly over the head. Remember to continue to use slightly heavier pressure at the bottom, and lighten your pressure as you get to the top.

Men, like women, sometimes only pay attention to the "up" stroke. However, there is as much sensation available on the "down" stroke as the up.

- Check and make sure he is feeling both the up and the down.

The Two-handed Method

Experiment by using both hands. Stroke up and down on his penis, one hand above the other, as if you were holding a baseball bat. Allow your top hand to slip off the top of his penis without losing contact with your bottom hand. Then slide both hands downward to the base of his penis and begin to come back up again. (See photo on the following page.)

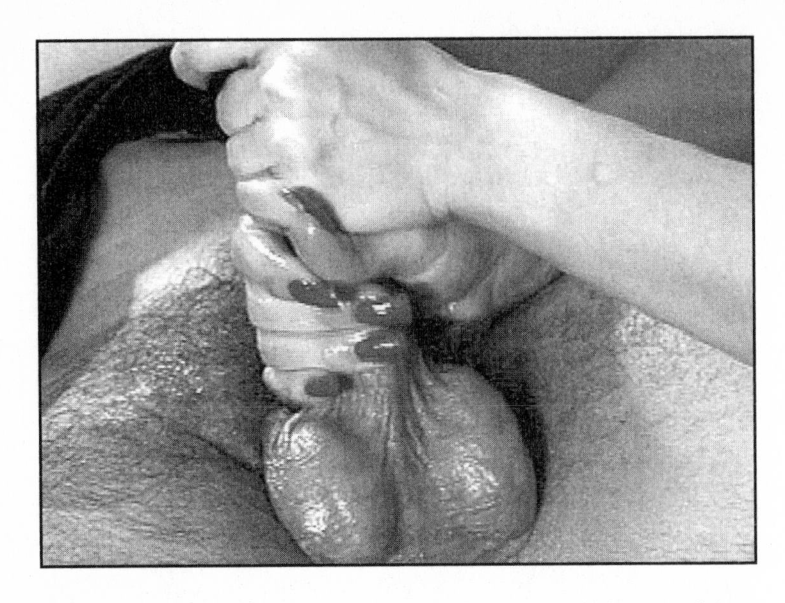

- As you feel his excitement begin to build up, either change the stroke, lighten the pressure you are using, or stop altogether. Remember, tell him what you are doing before you do it.

- Stroke different parts of his penis, including the sides, to discover what feels good to him.

- Experiment by altering the kind of strokes you use...faster, slower, firmer, lighter, shorter, longer, etc.

The Testicle Pull

Most women avoid handling their partner's testicles because they are afraid that they might hurt him. Normally men's testicles are very sensitive to pain, but at the high state of arousal that he has attained with your help, his testicles stop being sensitive to pain and begin to become sensitive to pleasure.

- Grasp him just above his testicles up close to his body by making a circle using the thumb and first finger of one of your hands.

- Gently begin to pull downward as you are stroking his penis with your other hand.

- With each degree of pull downward, check in with him to make sure he is feeling no discomfort. Keep gradually pulling downward without squeezing his testicles until you can pull no further, or until he says "enough."

Testicle pulling has another advantage. It can help your partner avoid ejaculation. Men usually aren't able to ejaculate unless their testicles are fully drawn up against their bodies.

Diagram Of The Male Genital Area

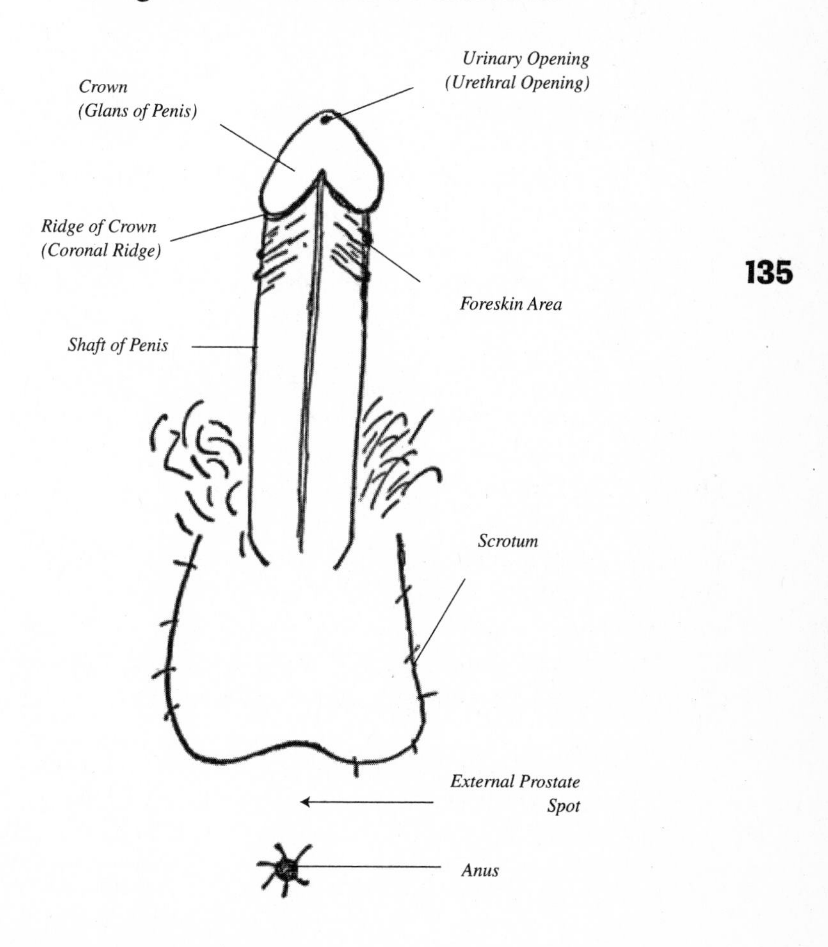

How You Can Add 1 to 3 Inches To His Penis

No one we have ever met has believed this was possible. Because of all of their skepticism, we even included a live demonstration of the technique in our video, ***For Her Eyes Only***.

This part of the "Venus Butterfly" technique is also very advantageous for the man both from a vanity, health, and pleasure standpoint. Also, it is a very easy skill for you to learn.

Here's the principle behind the technique. When a man looks down at his penis, whether soft or erect, all that he ever sees is about half of his equipment. The other half is the "root" of his penis. What we call his "buried treasure."

When you master the "Venus Butterfly" technique, you will be able to stimulate this hidden part of his penis. If you do it properly, it will become excited, swell up like the exposed part of his penis, and push everything out further.

There are also several practical reasons for learning this technique. This part of his penis, the perineum area, most likely has "virgin" nerve endings that have never been properly stimulated by anyone. You will probably be the first person who has ever done this to him. When done correctly, this technique will act like a turbocharger. It will increase his orgasm to heights he doesn't even know exist.

Another added benefit is that you are also stimulating his prostate. There is a lot of recent evidence that this is a healthy thing to do to him on a regular basis.

- As you are stroking his penis with one hand, reach between his bent legs with your other hand.

- Without touching him with your nails, use the tips of your fingers to feel the spot between his testicles and his anus. If he has an erection, it will feel like the semi-hard curved underside of his exposed penis.

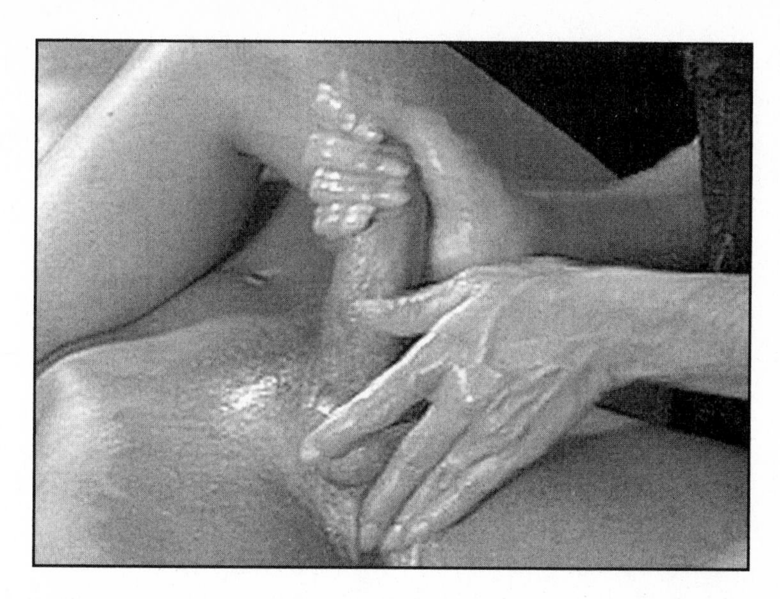

- With the tips of your forefinger and middle finger — being careful not to scratch him with your nails — stroke this area. Make sure the tips of your fingers go in the same direction, speed, and rhythm that your upper hand is using on his penis.

Use the "Training" or "Communication" cycle that follows to find out how much pressure and speed feels the best to him. You will probably find that he enjoys a great deal of pressure on this part of his penis.

The more pressure you use, and the faster your stroke, the faster will be his arousal. If you continue, he will most certainly ejaculate.

The "Training Cycle"

Your goal during this process is to give your partner the most intensely pleasurable feelings possible. The easiest way to accomplish this every time is to use what we call the More University "Communication" or "Training" Cycle. With this technique, you can find out where, when, and how to give your partner precisely what he wants, when he wants it, and for as long as he wants.

When you are doing the "Venus Butterfly" to your partner, you need to know at all times if you are hitting the correct spot with the right amount of pressure. The only way you can know this for sure is to ask, but you must be careful not to make your partner lose touch with what he is feeling.

By using the More University Communication or Training Cycle, you will learn the perfect amount of pressure and speed to use with each series of strokes, without having your partner lose the mood.

The secret is to ask simple, short, yes or no type questions which can be answered without too much thought. Here is an example:

1. "Would you like me to rub faster than this?" (Answer, "Yes.")

2. "Okay," you say as you increase the speed. "Would you like it faster than this?" (Answer, again "Yes.")

3. "Okay," you say as you increase the speed even more. "Would you like it faster than this?" (Answer, "No.")

4. "Okay. Would you like it slower than this?" (If you get a "No" at this point, you are at just the right speed. Just continue to use that speed. If you get a "*Yes*," continue to slow down until your partner lets you know not to decrease the speed any longer. At that point, you will know you are doing great.

This technique is very effective in helping you find the right spot on the penis or on any part of his body, and discovering which amount of pressure or speed feels best. "Would you like me to go slower?" ... "Would you like a lighter stroke?" ... "Heavier" ... "Harder?" ... "More lubricant?" ...etc.

Also, let him know that you want him to let you know immediately if there is anything you can do to please him more. Ask him if he would be willing to following just 3 simple steps?

1. At anytime that he wants you to do something different, the first step is for him to acknowledge your overall actions. He simply says, "That's great!" or "This feels so wonderful!"

2. Next, he makes a request of you that will bring him even more pleasure. It is a small step that you can easily fulfill. He could say, "Will you...(one of the following)

...go slower?" (faster?)

...stroke a little softer?" (harder?)

...come up a little higher?" (down a little lower?)

...stop for a moment?"

...give me a drink of water?"

...use more lubricant?"

By making a simple request, he is furnishing you with the information that you need so that you can give him exactly what will please him the most. This way you don't have to guess or shoot in the dark.

3. As soon as you respond to his request, then he says, "That's even better!" or "That's wonderful! Thank you."

Now you know that you are improving and that he appreciates your commitment to pleasing him. Each time, he makes a request, he follows *all* three steps. This is his version of the Training cycle when he is the one receiving pleasure.

Sex is one of the most difficult subjects couples attempt to communicate about. These Training cycles will help him communicate more easily and effectively about what feels best to him.

Connections

Now would probably be a good time to try to "connect up" other parts of his body with his penis. Basically, you are to rub on some part of his body which contains a large number of nerve endings and create a sympathetic response in his penis.

- An example would be his lips. Tell him you are going to begin to rub on his lips using a little lubricant at the same time you are stroking his penis.

- Once he is feeling pleasurable sensations in both areas, tell him that you are going to stop rubbing on his penis, but you want him to see if he can also "feel" the touching of his lips in his penis.

- After a while, inform him that you are switching back to his penis, and now you want him to feel your touching on his penis in his lips.

- Keep going back and forth until you have set up a connection between the two, or until this experiment stops being fun for either of you.

Some other time, try connecting up other areas. In future dates, make sure you have included all parts of his body. The most common areas that lend themselves favorably to being connected are the areas used in petting, such as his lips, neck, inside the mouth, his lower stomach, the inside or tops of his legs, and his chest and nipples.

Other areas with large bundles of nerve endings, such as the middle toe and the area around the anus, can also be explored on another "Venus Butterfly" date.

Take Him Over The Top

During your "Venus Butterfly" date, he may beg you to let him go over the top, but do not do this until you are ready for him to go. Tell him over and over that everything will be all right, just relax and maybe soon you are going to take him over the top. Hold out as long as possible.

- The most sensitive areas of his penis that quickly lead to orgasm will usually be the ridge of the crown or head of his penis, and the area on the underneath side of the base of the crown. Check how pleasurable it feels to him to be stroked in different directions at different speeds and pressures in these sensitive areas, as well as on the shaft.

- Switch to rubbing different parts of his penis. It will be pleasurable, but he will probably want you back on the most sensitive and pleasurable parts of his penis as quickly as possible.

Don't let him rush you. You are in charge and will get him there in due time.

Men can usually take less peaking than a woman. When you are starting out, a rule of thumb is to peak a man no more than three times.

- Remember to tell him what you are going to do before you do it. You might even use this opportunity to "peak" him some more. Sometimes, you can play with him in a way that increases his tumescence. Tell him that he has only twenty seconds to go over the top, and if he doesn't make it, you are going to bring him down one more time.

He will probably choke up under the pressure and not make it. That's fine. Every time you "peak" him, you build up the pressure of the climax and take it to a level that would not have been possible without peaking.

- As you feel his tumescence build to a critical point in his body and his penis, remind him to spread his fingers and toes to feel what you are doing to him all the way out to those areas. This allows him to spread the sensation and to feel whatever pleasurable feelings he is experiencing throughout his whole body.

All during your "Venus Butterfly" date, you should strive to get him to have orgasmic contractions and intense sensations without ejaculating. This is also the secret to a man's ability to have orgasms that last up to an hour.

Just remember, the ejaculation is not the orgasm for the man. The orgasm comes from the intense, pleasurable contractions that precede the ejaculation, and, with practice, you can cause him to have hundreds, even thousands of these contractions during a "Venus Butterfly" lovemaking session.

- As you continue and his tumescence builds, bring him as close to the edge as is possible without going over the top and letting him get into the ejaculation phase…then bring him down and regain control by trying one of the following methods: Stopping, Slowing way down, Changing to a much lighter pressure, Changing the direction you are rubbing, or Changing the rhythm you are using.

- Notice that each time you bring him close to the edge, the intensity of his contractions will increase. Continue to take him to the edge each time, and you will be able to keep his contractions and sensations going longer and stronger.

With enough practice, you will be able to get him to the top level of orgasm, which we call the "orgasmic state." At this level, he will be having full body contractions, one after the other, and you will be able to keep them going for as long as both of you want.

To reach this orgasmic state, you need to become proficient using the "Venus Butterfly" technique with total confidence. Also, his ability to feel and his nervous system will need to be strengthened so as to be able to reach high levels of intensity easily and without discomfort. Anyone can attain these abilities with enough practice.

A good "test" to see if he is paying attention to how much he is feeling is to tell him you are going to stop for just a moment.

- Immediately resume and do 10 strokes on him.

- Stop again and ask him how many strokes did he feel since you stopped a few moments ago. If he says 5, then he is only feeling 50% of the sensation that it is possible for him to feel.

Throw the "test" in every once in a while to check on his improvement.

- At some point he will either slip over the top, or you will deliberately take him there. Once he starts into the ejaculation phase, keep the rhythm and pressure you are using steady. Stay very alert to what you are feeling in your hand. You may need to begin to either lighten or increase the pressure you are using. Give him just enough pressure, but not too much.

You will learn as you practice how much pressure feels the best to him, and when to begin to lighten or increase your stroke.

You will notice that he will pull away from you if you are pressing too hard and push toward you if he wants more pressure.

- Here's the best part. Once he has climaxed totally and has nothing left, there are still pleasurable feelings left over for the taking. All you need to do is to continue to stroke him, using more Vaseline to smooth out the friction and probably a lighter and lighter touch as you bring him down.

- Bring him all of the way down. Do not leave him feeling like he is floating three feet over the bed. You will know you are finished when he is totally "flat." This means there are no more pleasurable sensations left in him.

- A good way to end with him is to lie on top of him. Heavy pressure on his body or chest will help bring him completely down .

At this point, if you have been allowing yourself to feel what he has been feeling, you may feel as if you have gone through the orgasmic state and climax yourself, and you may feel totally detumesced.

- Don't let up at this point. You are still in the process of making love to each other. Being intimate and talking is just as much a part of lovemaking as is touching each other. Have him tell you everything about how the whole "Venus Butterfly" date was for him from beginning to end. Get him to talk about even the smallest details and be specific as to what pleasurably sensitive areas you discovered on him.

You will be amazed at how much you continue to discover about each other and how new and exciting being with each other will become. Don't be surprised if you learn something new about each other each time you practice the "Venus Butterfly" technique…no matter how many years you have been together.

How'd You Do?

Well? Did you keep time? Did you keep his orgasmic contractions and sensations going for one hour this session?

Don't worry. He may even slip over the top too quickly sometimes. In the long run, it doesn't make much difference. How long you can get him to sustain an orgasmic state, or how many contractions you can get him to have, is really not that important.

The most important goal is to see how much pleasure and fun both of you can get out of practicing the "Venus Butterfly" technique.

Although being patient is easy when you are having fun, think of practicing the "Venus Butterfly" technique and training for one hour orgasms as if you were training to run a marathon.

If you were going to do a marathon, you would not jump up the first day and run 26 miles as hard as you could. You would start out with a mile or two at a slow pace. Later you would increase your distance until you got up to your goal. The same is true in mastering the "Venus Butterfly" technique.

Just keep practicing. Each time you do, you will find yourself going for more fun and pleasure.

You've Got It!

The information you have received so far, with practice, will enable you to produce dramatically extended periods of orgasmic contractions in your partner.

However, having an orgasm last an hour or more (no matter how exciting and thrilling the prospect) is not the primary purpose of the "Venus Butterfly" technique. It is a wonderful side benefit.

Our main goal is to teach couples how to have more fun in their relationships and their sex life.

In our videos/DVDs, ***For His Eyes Only*** and ***For Her Eyes Only***, you can see a live demonstrations of the "Venus Butterfly" technique being taught and successfully performed.

Good luck and have lots of fun every chance you get.

Notes

Chapter Twelve

Questions & Answers

Q. Who should be taken on the date first? The man or the woman?

A. Usually the woman should be taken on the "Venus Butterfly" date first unless the woman reads this book first and fears that her mate may resist if she tries to get him to read it. In that case she might just tell him that she is going to treat him to a very special "Date." After it is over, he will more than likely want more. That is the time to introduce her conditions for the second "date"— have him read the book or even watch the video/DVD, ***For His Eyes Only***. Make it as easy as possible for both of you to win.

Remember, men have very large and very, very fragile egos. It is important to let them know that there is nothing lacking or wrong with their sex technique. Your sex life is great. ***The One Hour Orgasm*** is only about having more fun and more pleasure.

Q. What if we don't have an hour or the energy for a one hour session?

A. Good question, and here is a great answer. It is called: ***The Three-minute Pleasure Break***

What if one or both of you are not really in mood or you only have a few minutes? If the most you can nudge your partner into is a couple of minutes, a few minutes will be perfect.

Sometimes time is a problem and other times neither of you are in the mood to consider any long pleasuring session or the pressure of producing a result for yourself or your partner.

Some couples lose their desire to make love from waiting too long. Waiting to pleasure yourself or your partner is like not eating for a long, long period of time. Eventually the strong cravings for food subside, but it is only temporarily. After a small amount of food, your appetite returns.

Here is what you should do:

1. Ask your partner to just give you three minutes. When they agree, look at the clock and begin.

2. Do whatever you can do to make your quick session as pleasant as possible, given your surroundings and short amount of time. Try not to go anywhere without at least a small tube of your Vaseline.

3. Do just the "Venus Butterfly" to your partner for exactly three minutes. At the end of the three minutes, stop and tell your partner that the three minutes that they agreed to are up. Ask if they want you to continue.

With my wife, Leah, I was amazed at how much extra available time and energy showed up on her part at the end of just three minutes.

Even if you need to stop at the end of three minutes, it was three more than you would have had if you had not started.

Also, you are peaking each other, building up the steam toward longer sessions.

Q. What if I ask my partner to do the "Venus Butterfly" to me and they say no?

A. Don't take it personally or let it throw you. The basic truth to why anyone says "no" to any offer is because they see a loss of something if they say "yes."

It is not the benefits they are saying no to, it is some part of the offer that they don't like or see as a disadvantage. If you make an offer to someone and the person rejects your offer, it is not you, but your offer that is being rejected. If you want someone to say yes, make them a better offer, but, first find out or try to guess what part of the offer the person is afraid of or doesn't like.

Ask which particular part of the offer they are saying no to. Another possibility is that the entire offer may not have been good enough. What if you offered to take someone out for dinner at McDonald's and they say no?

What would happen if you upped your offer? Would they now say yes? How about going with you tonight to their favorite restaurant?

Sweeten the offer you are making until they say yes.

Q. What if my partner is so tumesced that they won't let me get close enough to touch them in any way?

A. You may have waited too long. By the time either one of you is "tumesced" to the end of your rope, it is very difficult to bring up the idea of pleasure. If you let tumescence build up too high, you usually cannot do anything about it. It is like a fire that has gotten out of control. Sometimes you just have to back off and wait until it burns itself out.

The answer next time is to pay more attention to when tumescence starts to build up, begin to do something about it as soon as possible, and be pleasantly persistent.

The best answer we can give to men is to:

- be very compassionate;

- take all the blame and responsibility for having waited too long;

- ask her what she wants you to do to make up for what she is upset about and if it is at all reasonable, do what she wants as enthusiastically as you can;

- and continue to put all your attention on her, at least until the crisis is over.

Even if she wants you out of the room or the house, leave and keep thinking about her and what she would like next. From time to time come back to check on how she is feeling and ask if you can do this or that for her.

Keep showering her with your total attention. Giving someone your full attention is the most sure fire method for "detumescing" anyone. It doesn't matter that they know what you are doing. It still works.

Q. Why can't I just do the "Venus Butterfly" to myself rather than having to worry about a relationship?

A. Of course you *can*, but you cannot cause yourself either pleasure or pain to the degree that someone else can who is doing the same thing to you.

Can you imagine twisting your own arm hard enough to make yourself reveal government secrets?

Likewise, you cannot possibly give yourself the degree of

pleasure that someone else can, especially when both of your attentions are on just one of you.

It is like scratching an itch on your back. You can scratch yourself, but it feels so much better if someone you love scratches the itch for you.

Q. What happens if somewhere along the line of growing and getting more pleasure, we run into some problem that we aren't able to figure out? What do we do then?

A. Reach outside of yourselves for competent help or advice. A third party who is objective and has been where you are can offer some great solutions to what may seem like hopeless problems.

Couples should watch this video together when they are not feeling "connected."

Q. How do I find out more about *Diet's Don't Work*™?

A. Contact Diets Don't Work, Inc. by visiting www.dietsdontwork.net or call 866-NEVERDIET (866-638-3734).

Q. If I am not careful, will I ever ruin her climax by "peaking" my partner too long?

A. Probably, but it is not important. The goal is pleasure and to have fun together. A climax, although desirable, is great if it shows up, but it is not the end of the world if you miss a couple of times.

If she doesn't go over the top before your love-making session ends, you have actually peaked her one more time. The next time you do the "Venus Butterfly" to her, she will really have a head of steam built up.

Q. In our marriage, it is me that always wants sex and my husband is the one always saying no. What do I do?

A. Why do men say no to sex? Generally speaking, guys want sex, so when he says no to the woman he loves, something's wrong.

Of course, men say no to their partners for many of the same reasons she turns him down.

- Being tired
- Anger
- Not being in the mood
- Stress

Plus, we discovered that men had two additional reasons. The biggest reason we could find that a man said no to sex was because he didn't think, at the time, that he would be able to perform properly.

Of course, most men aren't about to readily admit something like this. They would usually make excuses like, "I have a headache," or "My back hurts."

Another reason that men confided that they turned down her advances was sports. Given the choice between sex and something that involves a ball, the ball thing seems to win most of the time.

If you are a woman, you will never again have to worry about the first five reasons listed above once you master the "Venus Butterfly" technique. You will be able to turn him on without any effort or energy on his part whatsoever and when you are able to do that, he will almost always accept your romantic offers.

Regarding the sixth reason, sports, we did come up with one idea in this area that really worked.

Q. What can I do when I want to be romantic, but my husband wants to watch sports?

A. We found a way that you can turn this "ball" problem into a lot of fun for both of you. Here's what we came up with:

- Make a wager that involves the "Venus Butterfly" that you both willingly agree to. If he wins, you will do what he proposes enthusiastically. If you win, vice versa.

- Have him make the two teams that are playing more evenly matched for betting purposes by giving points to one or the other. Then, you pick whichever team you want and he takes the other.

- The minute the game is over, the loser eagerly pays off the bet. No waiting. There needs to be *instant gratification* here, with no chance for welshing.

Just think. He will be thrilled that you are as intensely interested in the contest and the outcome as he is. You will be sharing one of his passions with him and as the game nears the end, the excitement and anticipation will build in both of you. There are no real losers. You both will have fun together, both during the game and at the pay off.

Q. Where do I go if I want to find out more info about how to win with my partner?

A. For more information please visit the following Web sites:

www.theonehourorgasm.com
www.dietsdontwork.net

Another possibility is to help yourself in the privacy of your own home by using our series of adult, sex education video tapes as described below:

Tape 1: For His Eyes Only... How To Make Sex More Fun For Her

This video is one of the best, most decent, tasteful, explicit, and effective adult romance and sex education videos ever produced for men. For the first time on video, several very different and attractive couples demonstrate "doing" the "Venus Butterfly" technique to a woman. This video brings *The One Hour Orgasm* to life for male viewers. It is filled with first-hand information that will improve any man's sexual effectiveness and his partner's sex life immediately.

- Improve your self confidence as a lover
- Increase the intensity and duration of her orgasms and cause her to have hundreds of orgasmic contractions
- Put the spark back, or prevent it from going away
- Bring back her sex drive
- Make every lovemaking session a pleasurable learning experience
- How even one inch of penetration can feel like twelve to her
- Solve the problem of not being in the mood at the same time

Tape 2: For Her Eyes Only...
How To Make Sex More Fun For Him

This video is one of the best sex education videos ever produced for women. For the first time on video, several very different and attractive couples demonstrate "doing" the "Venus Butterfly" technique to a man. This video brings *The One Hour Orgasm* to life for female viewers. It is filled with first-hand information that will improve any woman's sexual abilities.

- Improve your self-confidence as a lover
- Increase the intensity and duration of his orgasms
- Add 1 to 3 inches to his normal size
- Put the spark back, or prevent it from going away
- Bring back his sex drive
- Make every lovemaking session a pleasurable learning experience
- Learn "simulated" oral sex
- Solve the problem of not being in the mood at the same time
- Train his sexual nervous system to last longer

Tape 3: The Ultimate Valentine

Six romantic seductions to spice up any special occasion, including Valentine's Day, anniversaries, birthday, rainy weekends, or any time you just want to have some "special" fun! Featuring well-known models, including Griffen Drew from Playboy, and Penthouse magazine's Taylor St. Clair.

- Discover the "Velvet Touch" technique
- Learn how to inspire your Valentine to fulfill your wildest dreams!
- Get rid of your inhibitions, and use your Valentine's body to create the World's Sexiest Valentine!
- Discover your Valentine's hidden wild side
- Pamper your Valentine into fits of ecstacy!
- A *must-have* video!

Tape 4: The Ultimate Sexual Experience

Twenty years of incredible research by the nation's leading sex educators, Dr. Bob Schwartz and Dr. Leah Schwartz.

- Step-by-step to reaching sexual heights few even know exist!
- Is she really turned on?
- A "Touch of Ecstacy" that will leave her *breathless*!
- Footage never seen before of an incredible sexual phenomenon
- How even one inch of penetration can feel like twelve
- Learn to feel intensity you've never felt before
- Discover the common mistake most couple make
- The"Bread and Butter" stroke everyone is talking about

All four videos, in VHS or DVD formats, can be ordered by calling 1 (800) 227-1152 or directly from our Web sites, **www.theonehourorgasm.com** or **www.venusbutterfly.com**. If you wish to order more copies of ***The One Hour Orgasm***™, discount pricing is available on quantity orders.

If you are interested in losing weight and keeping it off for life, you'll want to order the *New York Times* best-selling book, ***Diets Don't Work! The Secrets to Losing Weight Step-by-Step When All Else Fails (New, Revised 3rd Edition*** by Dr. Bob Schwartz. ***Diets Don't Work!*** is recommended by universities and physicians all over the United States, Canada, and England. The book is only $12.95 (plus shipping and handling) and can be ordered by calling (866) NEVERDIET, or visiting www.dietsdontwork.net.

Your Personal Invitation

Workshops based on Dr. Baranco's teachings are held on weekends in the San Francisco area and frequently in major cities all across the country. If you would like a current schedule of courses or more information to help you have more pleasure in your life and your relationship, visit www.lafayettemorehouse.com or www.theonehourorgasm.com.

The Beginning

This is a book that you will want to read over and over. Each time you read it you can increase the amount of fun and pleasure in your life.

A Word of Caution

The final chapter in this book is very different from those which precede it. Chapter Thirteen talks about HIV/AIDS, the difference between "safer" and "survival" sex, latex gloves, triple barriers of protection, and a lot of other strange procedures and machinations.

It will be of little more than casual interest to those of you who are involved in committed, loving, monogamous relationships.

It *is*, on the other hand, of vital concern to those of you who are "single and loving it," and, for those carefree individuals, it may be the most important chapter in the book.

Remember, common sense is key!

Chapter Thirteen

Surviving "Safer" Sex

The advice contained in this book could not only help you find the perfect relationship, ***it can help you discover safer and yet completely pleasurable sexual experiences***.

The Survival Sex techniques which follow will not only bring pleasure to you and your future partner beyond your wildest dreams, it goes beyond what is now being inaccurately called "Safer" Sex.

The late Dr. Victor Baranco said that the "safer" sex recommended today falls very short of safe. He suggests that we go far beyond the methods being suggested at this time. He has come up with methods which are not only sensuous and pleasurable, but which we believe are also as careful as ideas others have come up with short of total abstinence.

His method, "Survival Sex," was designed for anyone who has

a partner who has had "intimate contact" with someone else within a five-to ten-year period.

"Intimate contact" is any circumstance where there was or might have been an exchange of body fluids, whether through sexual contact or not: intercourse, oral sex, deep kissing, blood, or sharp objects.

Intimate contact these days can be very scary. In some cases the deadly disease AIDS can be transmitted if a person has a cut (even one invisible to the naked eye), a rash, an abrasion, a broken blister or some other opening or weakness in the skin's epidermal barrier, and is exposed to infected blood or body fluids.* This book presents information about techniques that don't involve oral sex or intercourse and that not only provide much greater pleasure, but far less risk of pregnancy or disease. Oral sex, intercourse, and other intimate contact and associated safer sex practices are not topics intended to be addressed here. Given that these are activities that can pose greater risks, you should educate yourself before engaging in those activities.

If you are not absolutely certain that both you and your partner are totally free of sexually transmittable diseases, the technique called "Survival Sex" should be practiced.

*Research and knowledge about AIDS prevention continues to evolve as does debate and research about the use, effectiveness, and effects of nonoxynol-9 and other substances and agents. There are many resources available on the internet and elsewhere where you can find the most up-to-date information, such as the Centers for Disease Control and Prevention's Web site, http://www.cdc.gov.

Why?

Dr. William Masters and Virginia Johnson, in their book, ***Crisis: Heterosexual Behavior in the Age of AIDS***, talk about the potential for AIDS to also spread throughout the heterosexual community in epidemic proportions. Their research warns how lightly most of the heterosexual community, including the so-called experts, are taking this threat to human life. Masters and Johnson said that they believe that authorities are greatly underestimating the number of people infected with the AIDS virus in the population today. Six out of every hundred heterosexual people in a study they conducted were infected with the AIDS virus.

If 6 out of every 100 airplanes crashed, most of us would not fly. Even though their research was limited to a narrow group of heterosexuals who had multiple partners, it seems unreasonably dangerous and reckless not to take precautions and use common sense.

Some people who have the AIDS virus and transmit the disease to others appear healthy and may not even realize they are infected and so may not realize how particularly crucial it is to take precautions in terms of sexual behavior.

According to that Masters and Johnson study, the AIDS virus is working its way into the younger population—the 15 to 24 age group—the ones most susceptible to epidemics of sexually transmitted diseases because this group is the most sexually active.

The biggest reason AIDS still exists today is because of stubborn human behavior. Please seriously consider what we are about to suggest.

Sensuous "Survival Sex"

Sensuous "Survival Sex" begins with the familiar Boy Scout motto. *Be prepared* so that you and your partner will be as safe as possible and avoid the spread of disease and unwanted pregnancies without abstaining from sexing altogether.

The simple formula for Sensuous "Survival Sex" is:

1. Use a substance or agent that kills most sexually transmitted diseases.

This means that first you apply the prescribed amount of the creams or jellies (any lubricant with an anti-AIDS virus and/or sexually transmittable disease agent recommended by your health care professional).

Follow the instructions on the label and make sure that you cover any part of you which will be touching your partner. Your lips, hands, interior of your mouth, genitals, and any visible scratches or abrasions which may be exposed.

2. Use a barrier made of a substance such as latex.

When using the "Venus Butterfly" technique on a partner, slip into a pair of medical disposable latex examination gloves. These are thinner than latex surgical gloves and preferred for the sensual stimulation of the genitals.

These latex examination gloves are available in the sizes small, medium, large, and extra large at your local drugstore.

Make that snapping noise when you are putting them on so that your partner will begin to associate the sound to mean that "pleasure is on its way."

3. Put a second coating of the cream or jelly (not Vaseline) over the entire surface of the glove and then apply it to the areas of your partner which you are going to touch.

If the person being done is the man, it is further recommended that the penis be sheathed in a condom.

Now you are ready for what we believe is the best and relatively safest sensual experience you can enjoy giving your partner.

Complicated as this may sound, the whole procedure, if attentively and carefully done, can be incorporated into the pleasurable act and contribute to the sensuality of genital manipulation.

Warning: Do not use Vaseline if you are practicing "Survival Sex." Vaseline and other petroleum jellies contain properties which will melt and destroy the effectiveness of the material that examination gloves and condoms are made of.

If you are practicing "survival" sex, you have to use a non-petroleum type lubricant to keep friction from hurting your partner.

The Advantages To "Survival Sex"

During these times of widespread sexually transmitted diseases, the practice of unprotected sexual activity is foolish and life threatening.

Until you are prepared to risk life itself for the sake of a sexual encounter, it is advisable that sensual activity be limited to the expression of physical affection that clearly excludes the possibility of any direct contact with the genitals, semen, or any blood products.

Abstinence from sexual relations is the only real guarantee that one is totally immune from infection, however, the "Venus Butterfly" technique combined with Survival Sex precautions provide sensual pleasure, relieve the pressures of tumescence, and reduce the tendency to indulge in hazardous sexual activity.

It is also impossible to fully enjoy a sexual experience if one is worried about the possible fatal consequences of your sensual actions. Optimum sensual pleasure cannot occur if your mind is dwelling on disturbing images of disease, death, or an unwanted pregnancy.

One of the problems in the past with prevention methods is that we have had to apply them as quickly as possible after we had become aroused, and they were seen as a delay to pleasuring ourselves or our partners.

Correctly practicing the "Venus Butterfly" technique gives you all the time in the world to use Survival Sex to get ready.

If you are a man, and your partner knows that you are getting ready to pleasure her while she is lying on the bed in anticipation, everything you do that gets you closer to starting will add to her tumescent state. Your preparations can become a useful part of turning on your partner, as well as letting her know that you care enough about her to take precautions which could protect her from an unwanted pregnancy, keep her free of sexually transmitted diseases, and possibly *even save her life*.

Practicing "Survival Sex" is also a strong incentive to have a lifetime monogamous relationship with a loving partner who is trained to give you all the pleasure most people have only dreamed about.